JUSTICE ON BOTH SIDES

SERIES | RACE AND EDUCATION

Series edited by H. Richard Milner IV

OTHER BOOKS IN THIS SERIES

Urban Preparation
Chezare A. Warren

Truth Without Tears
Carolyn R. Hodges and Olga M. Welch

Millennial Teachers of Color
Edited by Mary E. Dilworth

JUSTICE ON BOTH SIDES

TRANSFORMING EDUCATION THROUGH RESTORATIVE JUSTICE

MAISHA T. WINN

Harvard Education Press
Cambridge, Massachusetts

Second Printing, 2018

Paperback ISBN 978-1-68253-182-2
Library Edition ISBN 978-1-68253-183-9

Library of Congress Cataloging-in-Publication Data
Names: Winn, Maisha T., author.
Title: Justice on both sides : transforming education through restorative justice / Maisha T. Winn.
Other titles: Race and education series.
Description: Cambridge, Massachusetts : Harvard Education Press, 2018. | Series: Race and education series | Includes bibliographical references and index.
Identifiers: LCCN 2018000296| ISBN 9781682531822 (pbk.) | ISBN 9781682531839 (library edition)
Subjects: LCSH: Restorative justice. | Reconciliation. | Community and school. | Teacher-student relationships. | Conflict management. | School discipline. | Teachers—Training of.
Classification: LCC HV8688 .W56 2018 | DDC 371.001—dc23
LC record available at https://lccn.loc.gov/2018000296

Published by Harvard Education Press,
an imprint of the Harvard Education Publishing Group

Harvard Education Press
8 Story Street
Cambridge, MA 02138

Figures 2.1 and 2.2 Design: Good on Paper Design
Cover Design: Endpaper Studio
Cover Image: ericsphotography/E+/Getty Images

The typefaces used in this book are Adobe Garamond Pro and Trade Gothic.

For Shakara and Niya

CONTENTS

SERIES FOREWORD

by H. Richard Milner IV
Race and Education Series Editor

Maisha Winn's *Justice on Both Sides* is essential reading for educators committed to justice and transformation—both provocative and timely as current discussions about race and education in contemporary society intensify. As Professor Winn notes, the book seeks to disrupt the ways in which the culture of mass incarceration permeates preK–12 education by building a case for a restorative teacher education. What Professor Winn proposes is a serious paradigm shift in thinking about how we prepare and support teachers so that they, in turn, can best understand and serve all students in their classrooms across the world. To that end, the book has a worthy and highly practical goal: to "prepare the next generation of teachers to be skillful restorative justice practitioners who disrupt educational inequities in classroom and school communities." *Justice on Both Sides* is a signature, urgent contribution to the Race and Education series. This is the book for which we have been waiting on a topic that needs and deserves more attention as our schoolchildren continue to be funneled into a criminal justice system that is not designed to promote democracy and humanity. Indeed, *Justice on Both Sides* challenges and compels us to educate rather than incarcerate. It is a call to educators to know more and to do better.

A central goal of the Race and Education series is to advance a critical, forward-thinking body of research on race that contributes to policy, theory, practice, and action. Although the series will advance scholarship in race and justice studies, a primary objective is to help educators—teachers, school counselors, leaders, coaches, and outside-of-school providers—center the humanity of students whose needs are far from being understood, responded to, and met in schools and in society.

Grounded in and substantiated by empirical research, the series aims to highlight effective practices designed to help solve intractable problems of race in education. To that end, books in the series address both societal challenges and educational equity. They highlight scholarship from leading researchers in the field as well as emerging scholars and investigate mechanisms, systems, structures, and practices that have a signifiant bearing on students' opportunities to learn.

Racial justice is arguably the most important educational imperative of our time. Considering the inextricable links between society and education, educators have the potential to help equip students with knowledge, tools, attitudes, dispositions, mind-sets, beliefs, and practices to create a world that is truly equitable and democratic for its citizenry. Thus, series titles attend to issues both inside and outside of schools as well as their nexus, shedding light on what matters and how we, in education, can improve practices that systemically improve students' opportunities reach their full capacity.

Above all, the Race and Education series asks the important question, *Do we have the fortitude to center race in our work, or will we continue going about our business as usual?* I am always mindful of curriculum theorist Beverly Gordon's provocative observation that "critiquing your own assumptions about the world—especially if you believe the world works for you"—is an arduous endeavor. At the very heart of this series is an explicit challenge to those in power to work for the good of humanity, to interrupt systems, policies, and practices that work only for some while others remain underserved. It asks: How do the effects of poverty and compromised opportunities in transportation, housing, and employment manifest themselves in communities' responses to social (in)justice? What role does and should education play in understanding and responding to these manifestations? What roles do teachers and other educators play in helping students develop insights about the salience of race in society? How do education policy makers respond to these realities when making decisions about what gets covered in the curriculum? The books in this series address many of these questions about race, racism, and discrimination to advance what we know (theoretically and empirically) in education and to move us toward a more equitable education system.

Indeed, a primary premise of the series is that we must learn from a diverse range of disciplines to build and sustain efforts on behalf of students who continue to be underserved and marginalized in education. Thus, scholars and scholarship from a variety of disciplines—sociology, psychology, health sciences, political science, legal studies, and social work—can assist us in reversing educational trends that continue to have devastating effects on student experiences and outcomes. There is solid evidence that students succeed when responsive and relevant mechanisms are in place. The Race and Education series will contribute to the educational equity and racial justice agenda, centralizing those mechanisms that will help us reach our true ideal democracy. I am ready. I am hopeful that readers of the series are as well.

Welcome! #LetsDotheWork!

INTRODUCTION

WHY WE NEED A PARADIGM SHIFT IN SCHOOLS NOW

In Spring Valley High School, in Columbia, South Carolina, a sixteen-year-old girl identified in some news reports as "Shakara" was asked to put away her cell phone during math class on October 26, 2015. When she did not comply with the classroom teacher's request, an administrator was called in and asked Shakara to leave the room. She did not. School Resource Officer Ben Fields, who is essentially an armed police officer, was asked to intervene. It was reported that Officer Fields told Shakara she was under arrest. What ensued—captured on video by the phone of a classmate—was Officer Fields grabbing Shakara by her neck while she was still seated and forcefully turning her desk over backward before dragging her across the floor as her peers watched helplessly or looked away. The adults stood at the front of the classroom and watched. One of Shakara's classmates, Niya Kenny, reportedly began shouting "What the F?" and praying aloud.[1] In the aftermath, the Richland County sheriff offered, "The student was told she was under arrest for disturbing school and given instructions which she again refused . . . the video then shows the student resisting and being arrested by the SRO [school resource officer]."[2] Niya Kenny told reporters, "I know this girl don't got nobody," when subsequently explaining her desire to interrupt the violence.[3] Both Shakara and Niya are African American; Officer Fields, the administrator, and the classroom teacher are White.

Officer Fields's response to Shakara's refusal to leave class is situated within the framework of South Carolina Code 16-17-420, also known as the "Disturbing Schools" statute, which states:

> It shall be unlawful:
>
> (1) for any person willfully or unnecessarily (a) to interfere with or to disturb in any way or in any place the students or teachers of any school or college in this State, (b) to loiter about such school or college premises or (c) to act in an obnoxious manner thereon; or
>
> (2) for any person to (a) enter upon any such school or college premises or (b) loiter around the premises, except on business, without the permission of the principal or president in charge.[4]

Like other laws throughout the United States, the language in the statute allows for ambiguous interpretation regarding how to identify, in practice, an action that is obnoxious or interferes with students or teachers.

Recognizing the dangers of this type of subjective practice, Governor Jerry Brown of California signed a bill in 2014, Assembly Bill (AB) 420, to limit the use of "willful defiance" as a rationale for suspending students; this rationale had been disproportionately used to suspend from school and remove from class students of color.[5] Underlying the change in approach outlined in AB 420 is the acknowledgment that something that is lawful is not necessarily just. It may have been *lawful* in South Carolina for Officer Fields to apprehend

Shakara, but it is certainly not clear that this outcome was *just*, in the sense of being morally right and fair.

There was much analysis of the footage from Spring Valley High, and varying opinions and interpretations regarding who (the student? the officer?) or what (the Disturbing Schools statute? Officer Fields's tactics?) was at fault, but little conversation about what I wanted to know and understand: Why did the adults present—a classroom teacher with sixteen years of experience and an administrator—feel the need to call the school resource officer into the classroom to deal with a student who was not physically threatening anyone in the classroom? Over the use of a cell phone! Was this standard protocol in this classroom community, part of the school culture, or both?

As a former classroom teacher, I vividly recall the first and last time I wrote a referral. I was a tenth-grade English teacher at my alma mater, and the assistant principal "of discipline" had a reputation for being verbally and psychologically abusive to students, a reputation he'd had since I was a student. Nothing had changed. When I checked in to set up my classroom in late summer, I received the school district syllabi, keys, and a thick pad of referrals. I recall laughing it off and thinking I would never use them. One month into fall semester, a student I liked very much, "Antonio," was having an exceptionally difficult time focusing and, more upsetting for me, was disturbing his classmates, who were starting to pay more attention to him than to me.[6] We exchanged words, and before I knew it I pulled out that referral pad and wrote him up. Antonio stood in front of me, looking very hurt, and said, "Really, Ms. Fisher [my maiden name]?" Then he stormed out. Everyone was quiet, the outcome I thought I wanted, but my own conscience was loud, as I knew I was sending this student to an administrator who had a reputation for being incredibly mean to students. I was paralyzed by my actions. How did I get to that point? Was writing him up necessary? Did I have another option? When this student returned to my class the next day, I offered him an apology in front of the class. I told my students that I wanted us to support one another and that I never wanted anyone to have to leave. Fortunately, Antonio did not harbor any anger toward me and simply expressed surprise that I had sent him out. "I thought we were cool," he said. In other words, he thought we had a relationship. And we did. However, for myriad reasons, I had defaulted to a practice at my fingertips that required no imagination or real teaching skill.

When I think about the thick pad of referrals I received as part of my onboarding process, I question how teachers are socialized into a system of injustice through practices that normalize removal and isolation. How can we reclaim our commitment to providing children and youth with intellectually stimulating learning environments that value their humanity while actively rejecting carceral responses to behavior problems that arise with children?

As a scholar and educator who teaches foundational courses for preservice teachers, I am interested in the contours of teaching, learning, and justice. My own questions about Shakara's experience became the impetus for *Justice on Both Sides*. What resources, other than arrest, were available to the administrators, teachers, and staff at Spring Valley High to address conflict in the classroom? How could the adults involved have responded differently? Why has it become standard practice to arrest students for such minor incidents? While this incident seems dated, because video and social media technologies now allow for the capture and immediate dissemination of images reflecting punitive and violent practices in American schools and communities, I argue that we have yet to pause and thoughtfully examine such patterns as stakeholders, particularly from the perspectives of new and seasoned teachers, school staff, and students. This strikes me as education malpractice and "business as usual" as an unconscious option.

ALTERNATIVE TOOLS, ALTERNATIVE OUTCOMES

Imagine that the Spring Valley High math teacher had decided that sending students out of his classroom was not an option and was instead committed to seeing each of his students as worthy, capable, and deserving of mathematical knowledge. Part of his work the first two weeks of each academic year was to facilitate restorative justice community-building circle processes in his classroom. Restorative justice circles, in the context of schools, are spaces for creating a participatory democracy or a movement toward "non-domination," requiring an "equal voice" for all shareholders or community members.[7] Imagine that on the first day of class, the teacher and his students placed their chairs in a circle, removing desks from the center so as not to obstruct eye contact. Once everyone was seated in a circle, the teacher introduced a small pyramid that his brother had given him to represent his journey as a math educator. The small pyramid, or "talking piece," was used to signal that the person holding it could speak and the others were invited to listen.

In the first "round" of the circle, the teacher asked students to respond to questions such as "Who are you?" and "Why are you here?" Some students said more than others, and a few passed on speaking altogether. In the second round, the teacher asked students to share personal experiences they'd had with math or math classes. During this round, students who passed the first time talked about how they disliked math and how it has always been hard for them, whereas others described math as one of their favorite subjects. Later in the week, the teachers and students circled up again for values and guideline exercises. These exercises served to establish what behaviors the students believed were important for the circle to function effectively. On index cards, everyone wrote three words or values they needed in order to be in relationship with others; they then circled one of the three to share with the larger group. Cards with words and phrases such as "respect," "being kind," and "patience" were placed in the middle of the circle on a centerpiece until everyone had a chance to share. The teacher underscored his desire to "be patient" with his students and for students to be patient with him. The value cards were placed on a bulletin board somewhere visible and accessible in the classroom.

Marcus Hung argues that using talk circles in math classes interrupts the more typical "stratified classroom talk," which is characterized by a few students dominating discussion and, consequently, benefiting most people in the class.[8] Hung, who initially used talk circles as a way of checking in with students prior to instruction, describes the moment a student suggested using talk circles for the entire class period so that "everyone can see everyone else" and feel a part of the mathematical community in their classroom.[9] Perhaps the teacher in the scenario we have imagined asked students to read an op-ed piece from the *New York Times* titled "Why Americans Stink at Math" in order to provocatively open doors for an honest discussion about math fears and successes.[10] Shakara and her classmates were in a remedial math class. Perhaps if the teacher had understood his work as including equity and access, and his own positionality as a White man, he might have considered sharing aspects of the Algebra Project, highlighting Bob Moses's commitment to positioning equity and access to algebra for Black children as a civil right.[11] Most importantly, imagine a bigger time and resource commitment from the school district to train all teachers, school personnel (including school resource officers), and administrators in restorative justice circle processes and to create opportunities for every professional in the education system to talk—across disciplines and roles—about race, class, gender, ability, and implicit bias, and about how these factors impact the work of educators and administrators.[12]

This line of thinking quickly moves into the domain of practice: What can teachers and school staff *do* to address discipline in their classrooms? How can classrooms be organized physically in ways that facilitate restorative justice? The concept of "justice" in restorative justice is the purposeful attempt to disrupt cycles of injustice and inequality. Although restorative justice can be defined in many ways, scholars consistently agree with criminologist and restorative justice theorist Howard Zehr that the premise "begins with a concern for victims and how to meet their needs, for repairing the harm as much as possible, both concretely and symbolically," and that it "involves a reorientation of how we think about crime and justice."[13] This requires making sense of who experienced the harm, how the harm affected people and relationships, and how stakeholders can seek a community response to the harm as opposed to fueling further polarization of those involved. This is difficult work, which is one reason why many schools lean on the language of restorative *practice* rather than restorative *justice*.

The harder work is establishing a mind-set or paradigm that views all children as valuable and worthy of affirming learning practices. This mind-set and paradigm insists that Black children, like Shakara and Niya, deserve, like all children, to be treated with dignity and respect. In an open letter to his son, *Between the World and Me* author Ta-Nehisi Coates describes how his desire to learn was interrupted by the reality of his schools: "The world had no time for the childhoods of black boys and girls. How could the schools? Algebra, Biology, and English were not subjects so much as opportunities to better discipline the body . . . I was a curious boy, but the schools were not concerned with curiosity. They were concerned with compliance."[14] The focus on compliance in schools is dehumanizing; it does not require educators to see students as fully human and capable of learning, engaging, or having curiosity. Most learning communities that focus on compliance serve Black, Latinx, and Indigenous children. "Urban pedagogies," according to Garrett Duncan, forsake rigorous teaching and learning for a desire to control students who are deemed to be in need of harsh discipline.[15] These norms teach teachers that Black and Brown bodies in schools are disposable and that Black and Brown children are essentially "nobody," making them easier to isolate, kick out, and push out, rather than to bring in, support their learning needs and goals, and take time to get to know them and their interests.[16]

Kay Pranis asserts that in order to fully grasp the shift in worldview that restorative justice requires, one would need to cultivate a "restorative impulse." An education team that uses restorative impulse might approach challenges from the vantage point of "we cannot drop out, kick out, or get rid of anything. We must deal with one another and with our environment. From this worldview, 'getting rid of' is *never* a solution because we are never really rid of anything—we are always connected."[17] So let's say Shakara has been told to put away her cell phone more than once. The teacher reminds her that that the word or value she offered to the circle on the first day of class was "respect." After this reminder, he and Shakara discuss what "respect" means to them both. Perhaps Shakara says the teacher's tone was "disrespectful" or lets him know she is dealing with an emergency with a family member and her parents have asked her to keep her phone close. Maybe the teacher explains that he is concerned that her cell phone might stand in the way of mathematical knowledge that is foundational to her math trajectory at school and beyond. If he learns there is a family emergency, he may offer to keep her cell phone out on his own desk and promise to check it periodically to confirm that no urgent calls come in during class.

Though this is hypothetical, it underscores how dynamics change when a restorative justice paradigm is in place, because creating and sustaining positive relationships is situated at the core of the work of teaching and learning.

If I use this lens to think about how I responded to Antonio, I realize that I ignored the restorative impulse I had to never send students to an assistant principal with a reputation for being unfair and unkind. A restorative impulse would have made me stop to consider the implications for sending a Latinx student to an assistant principal who was eager to punish. After I uttered the word "referral," it almost began writing itself. I felt too embarrassed to retract and was far more concerned with what the other students thought than with taking responsibility and demonstrating that one's initial reaction is often not the best. Practicing restorative impulse would have led me, instead, to speak to Antonio one-on-one to remind him of our mutual respect. I would have asked him to honor this mutual respect and reminded him of my own commitment to keep every student in the classroom learning. This would have taken the same amount of time as confronting Antonio with the referral. Knowledge of restorative justice and a framework for practice might have allowed me to link impulse and mind-set with appropriate action.

WHY RESTORATIVE JUSTICE IN SCHOOLS? WHY NOW?

The outcome at Spring Valley was not atypical. Classroom teachers across the country contribute to a daily cycle of isolation or removal of students under the umbrella of "zero-tolerance policies" that mandate specific, consistent, harsh punishment for rule breaking, regardless of the circumstances, reason for the behavior, or student's history. Data from the US Department of Education's Office for Civil Rights demonstrate that specific student populations experience disproportionate amounts of zero-tolerance policies; they are overwhelmingly Black, Latinx, Indigenous, and differently abled, and are being isolated and pushed out as early as preschool.[18] Black girls are the fastest-growing population to experience zero-tolerance punishment in American schools,[19] and differently abled and special education students are being either physically restrained or restrained with devices designed to "immobilize or reduce the ability of a student to move."[20]

Scholars often trace zero-tolerance policies to the tragic 1999 Columbine High School shooting. Columbine High School is in a suburban Colorado location serving predominantly White students, and the two murderers were White students, but most of the zero-tolerance policies subsequently enacted throughout the country were rolled out in urban public schools that served non-White students.[21] Recent scholarship points out, however, that schools serving black students began to include police presence as early as the 1950s.[22] As more data related to school discipline and the racial disparities of how suspensions, expulsions, and other mainstream forms of isolation are enforced in school settings become available, school communities are coming under pressure to disrupt these trends. However, in many instances, teachers are being asked to cease old practices without being introduced to new tools or alternative paradigms.

Zehr asserts that, rather than a finite set of practices, restorative justice is a paradigm shift. His seminal book, *Changing Lenses*, first published in 1990, challenged those who identify as "Christian" to rethink their investment in a retributive mind-set. In the twenty-fifth anniversary edition of *Changing Lenses*, Zehr identifies racial justice as being central to restorative justice and highlights mass incarceration as one example of the country's inability to focus on how harm—and the criminal justice system response to harm—negatively impacts everyone.[23] Civil rights attorney and cofounder of Restorative Justice for Oakland Youth, Fania Davis, similarly argues that everyone suffers when justice is ruptured. She describes restorative justice as a worldview that privileges human relationships:

> Restorative justice is founded on a worldview that affirms our participation in a vast web of interrelatedness. It sees crimes as acts that rupture the web, damaging the relationship not only between the individuals directly involved but also vibrating out to injure relationships with families and communities. The purpose of [restorative justice] is to repair the harm caused to the whole of the web, restoring relationships to move into a brighter future.[24]

Both Davis and Zehr assert that human relationships must be examined from all angles using a lens that seeks to think about how everyone is connected. For example, each of Shakara's classmates now has personal experience with the threat of violence in a space of formal learning. Education professionals who do want to create strong relationships with students and their families now suffer as well, because many of these students and families feel they cannot trust the adults in the school. If we think about schools as a vast web of interrelatedness—students, teachers, social service providers, administrators, administrative staff, coaches, janitorial staff, cafeteria workers, bus drivers, parents/guardians, and, in some cases, police officers—we understand that they come to the space for different reasons but should be grounded in a paradigm that values the lives and contributions of every stakeholder.

The purpose of this book is to offer a theory of restorative justice in education and to map pedagogical stances that support restorative, transformative justice discourse and practice. The book examines how a restorative justice paradigm shift might change how we conceptualize and administer punishment, shame, and guilt to reflect a more nuanced understanding of harm, the needs of those harmed, and those who have caused harm. It also describes restorative justice tools that can support *all* youth and their teachers in cultivating participatory democracy, which should be a function of public education in the United States. To this end, *Justice on Both Sides* is guided by the following questions:

- What role, if any, can restorative justice play in creating a participatory democracy in which teachers and students can practice justice in classrooms and schools?
- How do students view the work of restorative justice? How does school staff view the work of restorative justice? What are the tensions and possibilities for restorative justice in classroom and school communities?
- How do we prepare the next generation of teachers to be skillful restorative justice practitioners who disrupt educational inequities in classroom and school communities?

AUDIENCE FOR THIS BOOK

As I imagine my audience, I see myself setting a table for stakeholders such as students and their parents; classroom teachers; teacher educators, like myself; restorative justice practitioners; and equity-oriented scholars who might be well-established or emerging, trying to make sense of this practice called "restorative justice" (RJ) and determine whether it has a place in school settings. Around this table I would strategically situate my guests to ensure that no two guests who share the same position or positionality in terms of career, jobs, and so forth are seated next to each other. This communal table would be, for all of us, an opportunity to learn with and from one another. As I envision the participants in RJ circle processes, I imagine the audience for this book to be a group of stakeholders in a circle process that gives them time and supportive space to learn and unlearn. This book is written with educators in mind—educators being those who engage with children and youth in school settings, in various capacities—and those who shape and influence young people's minds. This book is also written for those who have the power to change the life experiences of children, through action or inaction—administrators and policy makers at school and district levels who have opportunities to influence policies and practices that impact children and their families. And, finally, this book is also written for my RJ colleagues who train others and facilitate circles but have not taught in schools.

NAVIGATING THIS BOOK

Restorative justice theorists often position restorative justice as a "compass" as opposed to a map. A compass is a tool that offers direction; a map helps one determine the best route. *Justice on Both Sides* seeks to do both: it offers direction for the work of engaging a restorative justice mind-set or paradigm while orienting the reader to youth perspectives. It then outlines several best practices that have emerged from the practice of restorative justice in schools, with the aim of helping readers imagine possible routes relevant to their own context. Chapter 1 describes the restorative justice paradigm and its characteristics. Chapter 2 outlines pedagogical stances for teachers who want to engage in RJ work, emphasizing the need to develop responsible discourses that support teaching and learning communities. Chapter 3 is an invitation to think about RJ work through the perspectives of students who have been trained in restorative justice circle facilitation. Chapter 4 draws from the experiences of a range of educators involved in justice-seeking work—a coach, a school psychologist, a dean of students, a classroom teacher, and an assistant principal. To better capture the arc of RJ work and its nuances, chapter 5 examines the tensions and challenges of restorative justice in schools and looks specifically at how restorative justice and justice-seeking work becomes the responsibility of women, girls, and people of color. Chapter 6 maps a Transformative Justice Teacher Education (TJTE) agenda, a call to action for preservice and in-service teachers who want to practice justice in their learning communities. Throughout the book, I serve as a paradigm shift communicator, signaling our need for transformative approaches that disrupt inequities in schools while we seek to support all students and educators.

CHAPTER 1

PARADIGM SHIFTING ON BOTH SIDES

The Art and Science of Making Things Right

BECOMING A "PARADIGM SHIFT COMMUNICATOR"

When I first started considering the relationship between restorative justice and education, I had a conversation with two restorative justice attorneys, sujatha baliga and nuri nusrat,[1] whom I shadowed at the National Council on Crime and Delinquency and later at Impact Justice in Oakland, California, so that I could learn more about restorative justice from a legal perspective. baliga, at the time, was one of the country's leading restorative justice attorneys and known for her restorative justice facilitation in a capital murder case in Florida in which the family of a young woman who was murdered by her fiancé requested a restorative justice process.[2] nusrat's work focused on sex crimes in schools, and she was a strong advocate for sex and sexuality education in schools. Sia Henry, also an attorney, was keenly interested in criminal justice reform for nonviolent drug dealers.

During one of our many "visioning" meetings, where we dared to dream of systems that both restore and transform, these women expressed how much easier it was for them to work on capital cases than to work with schools. As a former teacher, education researcher, and teacher educator, I was startled by their preference for capital cases over schools. Probed further, baliga offered, "With capital cases, you know what to expect . . . and you also understand the scope of your work. Schools often ask us to come in after so much harm has already taken place, and it's difficult to wrap your mind around how children are treated as well as how things got so bad."[3] But the bigger problem was that schools were required to follow punitive discipline processes in tandem with "doing" restorative justice, or RJ, which meant those traditional processes could undermine restorative justice. In other words, for a school to operate under a restorative justice paradigm, it must abolish the suspension and expulsion process and use restorative justice processes to respond to harm.

If suspensions and expulsions are an option, they will be exercised, because they do not require anyone to change or challenge established views or practices. No one is required to sit in the difficult space of revisiting something that they have always seen done. The option of suspensions and expulsions compromises and even corrupts the restorative process. nusrat also observed that "there are too many harm circles in schools" and that the way restorative justice is being carried out merely replicates the criminal legal system and causes more harm. Both nusrat and baliga have borne witness to the other side of punishment, so to speak, when people subjected to years of miseducation and consequently harmed by the schooling process, as well as other societal factors, found themselves replicating aspects of the harm they experienced by harming others. The two women questioned how and why school communities allow relationships between students and teachers or other adults in an educational setting to become damaged and why schools are unable to disrupt this pattern before it evolves into seemingly irreparable harm.

My work as an equity-oriented scholar examining how Black and Latinx students are labeled, sorted, and often deemed unworthy, and the impact this has on their opportunities and abilities to imagine their futures, fueled my desire to learn how restorative justice could respond to a history of injustice for historically marginalized children in American public schools. While I was determined to learn about restorative justice from lawyers like nusrat, baliga, and their partner, Sia Henry, who engage in this work daily, I also needed more training in various aspects of restorative justice to inform my work in education. My first charge was to spend as much time as possible with restorative justice practitioners and, when I could, to complete their trainings, including baliga's Restorative Justice Building Community training; Restorative Community Conferencing training with Impact Justice; Repairing Harm training at the Restorative Justice Training Institute with Rita Alfred; and a Restorative Justice and Trauma-Informed Practices training with Millie Burns in Richmond, California. After spending one year with RJ practitioners in out-of-school contexts, I realized how dangerously close I was as a researcher to misunderstanding this entire restorative justice thing. My introduction to restorative justice was in school contexts where it was being used as an alternative to school discipline policies such as in-school and out-of-school suspensions and expulsions. When I started following the work of restorative justice in 2012, its use seemed to have progressed; schools had started reducing the numbers of students being suspended and expelled. However, racial disparities in suspensions and expulsions persisted, and relationships between many students and teachers worsened, with teachers feeling as if students were getting away with questionable behaviors and not being held accountable for their actions.

It wasn't until I immersed myself in the daily practice of restorative justice that I learned that its objective is to build community and cultivate relationships among a group of stakeholders. It is about equity, understanding context, and true accountability, in which everyone acknowledges their responsibility to humanity and makes a commitment to putting things right when they have caused harm. According to my colleague Rita Alfred, reducing suspensions and other forms of isolation can only happen once we find value in relationships. My time with nusrat, baliga, and Henry was also when I began to really understand restorative justice as a paradigm as opposed to any set of practices or a specific program. That is, to practice restorative justice, one must not only be committed to seeing the full humanity of others but also be open to the possibility of not always being right but instead *making things right*. People accepting Fania Davis's assertion that we all participate in a "vast web of interrelatedness" would be a great beginning. Restorative justice is not merely an alternative to punishment; it is a way of life, and it can be difficult to ignore our instincts and not determine in advance whether someone is worthy of our attention and grace. Elsewhere I argue that it is much easier to believe that people in prison and children who underperform in school are perpetually wrong, because it absolves us of our debt and role in making things right.[4]

If restorative justice is a paradigm shift—and I believe it is—then my objective as a scholar, teacher educator, and RJ practitioner is to be what baliga calls a "paradigm shift communicator." Her team's primary audience includes district attorneys, public defenders, judges, juvenile justice service providers, and other lawyers; my primary audience includes teachers, teacher educators, administrators, and students and their families. I do not enter this work as someone who merely studies and theorizes restorative justice from a distance. I enter it as a human being who has been transformed by restorative justice and its many processes by learning how I have both experienced and caused harm (no easy task). I am now constantly pondering how to think restoratively or to cultivate a "restorative impulse."

To respond with a restorative impulse takes practice, and classroom teachers and other educators in school buildings need and deserve the time it takes to really understand this work and its potential along with why it is so valuable. Most importantly, all children in America's schools deserve to be given a chance to be honored as human and teachers need new tools that build their capacity to embody and enact this value. To this end, *Justice on Both Sides* is my attempt to communicate this paradigm shift and serve as a meeting point for classroom teachers, RJ practitioners, administrators, and students and their families.

THE THREE PILLARS OF RESTORATIVE JUSTICE

In the *Little Book of Restorative Justice*, Howard Zehr attempts to distill the salient characteristics of restorative justice, including what he refers to as the three pillars of RJ: harms and needs, obligations, and engagement.[5] Below I describe how these pillars of RJ can be applied to, and particularly useful in, school settings.

Harms and Needs

One of the reasons it is challenging to create a restorative justice culture in schools is because it is difficult to assess who has caused harm, who has experienced harm, and whose needs should be addressed. Most recently, RJ theorists have called for restorative justice to do more to address the needs of those who offend or cause harm. I argue that many of the students who cause harm in schools have also experienced harm in schools, through miseducation, constant surveillance, isolation, and discrimination. For example, Damien Schnyder argues that Black students in American public schools are often subjected to "educational enclosures," meaning that many school communities reflect "prison-base[d] logic that demand[s] the reproduction of racialized, gendered, and sexed hierarchies through multifaceted enclosure projects."[6] According to Schnyder, the term "enclosures" (as opposed to the more commonly used "school-to-prison pipeline") conveys the historical trajectory of challenging or denying Black independence and freedom. In his case study of one school in Southern California, Schnyder found "'non-visual' trapping that was representative of the most insidious enclosure within the school; the attempted denial of Black autonomous spaces of being."[7] In sum, tangible artifacts challenge the freedom of Black students in many schools, as do policies and practices suggesting that Black students are not worthy of experiencing freedom. Fania Davis asserts that the United States should engage in a truth and reconciliation process using restorative justice to come to terms with the ongoing violence against Blacks. Such a process, she suggests, would be "ongoing" and "collective."[8]

As a group, teachers and other education professionals have, in many cases, also experienced harm (many feel devalued, most receive low pay, many experience strained relationships with administrators, etc.) and have needs that must be considered. It often feels difficult to ask educators to do any more than they already do. Elsewhere I argue that, at minimum, teachers must be paid to complete RJ training and must receive ongoing support.[9] I have also argued that it would be ideal to train preservice teachers in RJ theory and circle process facilitation during their teacher education program (an idea I discuss in depth in chapter 6). Rather than offering classes in "classroom management," teacher candidates should receive in-depth training accompanied by readings and experiences to prepare them to think restoratively and create transformative learning spaces. If teachers are prepared to think about access to languages, literacies, the sciences, history, art, music, and mathematical reasoning as both civil and human rights, it might be possible for them to think about the moral and ethical obligations of addressing harms and needs that stem from education debt.

In a restorative justice process, all stakeholders have an opportunity to explore "What were your needs before the incident in question?" and "What are your needs now?" Imagine students, youth, and adults in a school community discussing their needs to address obligations and next steps to make things right, from the very beginning of the academic year, and determining together who is obligated to meet these needs.

Obligations

While critics of restorative justice in schools often posit that children are no longer being held accountable for their actions, this signals to me a lack of understanding and training in the RJ field. In restorative justice, accountability and responsibility are central in responding to harms and needs. I often ponder why people think suspensions, expulsions, and other forms of isolation are effective means of holding children accountable. If that were true, K. Wayne Yang argues, "Crudely speaking, more discipline should result in more achievement."[10] We know, though, that the "punishment gap"—to borrow from Yang—produces the opposite.

When a school community views its work through justice- and freedom-seeking lenses, stakeholders see this work as an obligation to children and the future. Some of the challenges of such work include the default impulse to blame parents and families for what teachers, administrators, and the public tend to view as deficits rather than focusing on how the school community can build capacity. Creating a culture of self-discipline for students and educators is one way to think about obligations in an education context.

ENGAGEMENT. Engagement is the opportunity to practice justice and freedom while cultivating participatory democracy. In pure restorative justice contexts, engagement or participation can be achieved through dialogue, conferences, or even indirect exchanges. According to Zehr, "The principal of engagement implies involvement of an enlarged circle of parties as compared to the traditional justice process."[11] A classroom community committed to the four pedagogical stances outlined in this chapter will insist on engagement; members of such classroom communities usually come to recognize the intrinsic incentives associated with doing this work—participants want to be part of a respectful learning environment, and they want to belong when they feel valued.[12]

DOES RESTORATIVE JUSTICE THEORY MATCH REALITY?

Not yet. However, I am hopeful. While the end goal of restorative justice in a school context should be to cultivate a sense of purpose and belonging by identifying harms and needs; understanding whose obligation it is to address these harms and needs; and creating opportunities to become engaged participants of a community with shared values and guidelines, it is primarily being used in school contexts as an alternative to punitive discipline policies. In other words, restorative justice, as being practiced in schools, is generally closer to the caboose than to the engine driver controlling the destination. Ideally, restorative justice will be used to cultivate a shared vision of how people in a school should be in relationship with one another while shaping a school's values and guidelines for interactions. Some scholars advocate that we "apply principles of restorative justice more aggressively to school settings" in order to decenter punitive approaches to harm.[13] Arguing that the purpose of public education is to prepare students for democratic engagement, William Haft asserts that the punitive approach that is endemic to American school culture "runs directly counter to a fundamental purpose of public education—the purpose of preparing children to live in a democratic society."[14]

What would it look like to educate children in American public schools for civic engagement? And what if school communities saw such civic engagement as part of the work of schools? When school communities embrace restorative justice as a paradigm, students are introduced to a restorative justice culture in which they are supported and encouraged to expand and deepen existing relationship skills or are offered tools to help them work on establishing and maintaining healthy relationships. Some school districts have started to give it a try. Oakland Unified School District (OUSD), in California, implements restorative justice in its schools, with a primary focus on building community. One key finding in the OUSD report is that restorative justice has built "developmental assets": "Students in restorative justice circles report enhanced ability to understand peers, manage emotions, greater empathy, resolve conflict with parents, improve home environment, and maintain positive relationship with peers. They are learning life skills and sustainable conflict management skills."[15] While OUSD has been transparent about challenges, including the need to train parents in restorative justice so that they could fully participate in the process, the district has not only made a commitment to continue to improve its work with middle and high school RJ coordinators but also plans to establish elementary school RJ coordinators.

Though OUSD reports that their school communities have benefited from restorative justice, many districts claim the opposite. In Fresno Unified School District (FUSD), in the Central Valley of California, school leaders adopted restorative justice with the aim of reducing the disproportionate numbers of Black and Latinx students being suspended and expelled.[16] One teacher at Fresno's McLane High School maintained that "the programs have backfired" and claimed that students are no longer being disciplined. Teachers at McLane generated a petition in which they assert, "When students face no accountability measures, it undermines the authority of all teachers, and creates a negative campus culture."[17] The language in this petition is revealing. I would argue that teachers at McLane have not been trained in restorative justice, because accountability is central to the work of restorative justice. These claims show that the school has not yet adopted a restorative justice mind-set or paradigm; rather than teachers asserting authority over students, a restorative justice paradigm requires that they learn how to be in relationship with students and establish mutual respect and accountability. Accountability is not solely the responsibility of students; educators, too, must be held accountable for their actions and interactions with students. Another teacher, who had been at McLane for eleven years, acknowledged that "restorative justice can work, but it's not being implemented correctly at McLane."[18]

In 2014 the Madison Metropolitan School District (MMSD) in Madison, Wisconsin, implemented a new policy known as the Behavior Education Plan (BEP). Naming restorative practices and restorative conversations as part of its overall objective, the BEP made it more difficult for teachers to send students out of their classrooms for whatever they deemed worthy of isolation or removal. However, a mere eight weeks into the 2014–2015 inaugural year of BEP implementation, an article in the *Wisconsin State Journal* titled "Madison Teachers: New Discipline Policies Not Working" claimed that "a new, less punitive approach to student discipline has resulted in serious behavior problems that schools are not equipped to handle."[19] According to the article, an MMSD middle school teacher explained in her interview, "The theory does not match the reality." An elementary school teacher acknowledged that "the school-to-prison [pipeline] is a real thing . . . [and] the BEP looks great on paper, but we don't have the staffing to carry it out effectively." While acknowledging that schools enact policing and surveillance of Black, Latinx, and "Other" students that create a school–prison nexus, this teacher was not convinced that she and her colleagues were responsible for dismantling these practices because of staffing issues. Restorative justice, then, had become a tool to respond to racial disparities in school discipline policies and practices, which is not the same as shifting to a worldview that values all students.

A *New York Times Magazine* profile of a high school in New York City and efforts therein to change school culture, titled "An Effective but Exhausting Alternative to High School Suspensions,"[20] detailed the journey of a principal considered in 2011 to be an "early adopter" of restorative practices. The principal, Phil Santos, described restorative practices as "exhausting" and "messy" while acknowledging that "changes in teacher attitudes and student behavior come slowly." However, despite the obstacles, Santos was committed to this work and forged ahead in advocating for a restorative culture in his school community.

This notion of "changes in teacher attitudes" is the gap this book aims to fill. Desired outcomes for administrators often run counter to what teachers need and want. Administrators often want to decrease the number of suspensions and expulsions, seeing it as a bonus if racial disparities dissipate as well. However, attempting to reduce suspensions without giving educators alternative tools does not build community. The tensions reported in districts such as MMSD and FUSD demonstrate that a school must do more than announce, "We're doing restorative justice now." If restorative justice is a paradigm and not a program, educators need pedagogical stances or ways of positioning themselves and their work so that they can engage effectively in the process.

HOW RESTORATIVE JUSTICE ENGAGES "BOTH SIDES"

What does it mean for restorative justice practitioners to consider justice "on both sides?" Why this binary? Is there a third side? A fourth? *Justice on Both Sides* refers to how students perceive relationships between students and teachers. Part of my work in trying to understand restorative justice in school contexts included immersing myself in one school community that trained several administrators, student services staff, and students. I interviewed students and staff in a Midwestern high school, Kennedy High School,[21] that trained its students to be restorative justice circle keepers (described in chapters 3–5). One student circle keeper, "Viola," a twelfth-grade, college-bound, African American student at the school, offered this definition of restorative justice: "[Restorative justice] is making the wrongs right, but making it right in a way that both sides can come to an agreement. 'Cause there's some justice where it's just like, 'I feel like this is justice,' but that other person might not agree. Restorative justice . . . is like you're restoring an issue and it's justice on both sides, and they've come to that agreement that this is what's gonna happen" (May 8, 2014). I shared this quote with nusrat, baliga, and Henry, who live and breathe this work. They thought it was the best definition they had heard, and I have referenced it widely. Viola experienced academic success but could not ignore the fact that many of her African American peers had not. Furthermore, she witnessed African American peers being subjected to punishment more often and to a greater extreme than any other ethnic group in her school. As an RJ circle keeper, Viola took her work seriously and wanted to maintain balance between the "student side" and the "teacher side."

A restorative justice circle process thus has the potential to bring students and adults together by having participants respond to a series of questions that encourage participants to describe how they have experienced harm, which allows everyone involved to hear one another, often for the first time; to explore the needs of everyone involved; and to collaboratively identify potential pathways to make things right. In other words, the RJ circle provides a forum for exploring histories, futures, tensions, and paths forward. In such a process, educators and the students they serve no longer assume oppositional "sides"; indeed, restorative justice seeks to undermine such binaries. In addition to giving a more thorough explanation of restorative justice circles and how they are used, I outline the pedagogical tools that ground an RJ paradigm shift in chapter 2.

CHAPTER 2

HISTORY, RACE, JUSTICE, AND LANGUAGE

Four Pedagogical Stances to Practice Restorative Justice

"If she had not disrupted the school and disrupted that class, we would not be standing here today," said Richland County sheriff Leon Lott after reviewing the footage showing Officer Fields throwing Shakara down and dragging her across her classroom. Sheriff Lott went on to explain: "So it started with her and it ended with my officer. What I'm going to deal with is what my deputy did."[1] In the aftermath of the Spring Valley High incident, debates over whether Shakara did something to deserve a violent response intensified. Officer Fields had supporters who knew him in different contexts and were shocked by the video footage, claiming that it did not tell his full story. Though Sheriff Lott avoided questions about if and how race factored into this case, many questioned whether Officer Fields would have responded the same way had Shakara been White. Even the notion of what it means for a student to be disruptive or to disturb a classroom or school was debated. Throughout these discussions, Shakara's integrity was challenged by those who thought she deserved her fate because she had not complied.

Approximately two years prior to this incident, Minnesota Public Radio invited me to speak on the topic "Why don't we talk about young Black females?"[2] I was joined by Monique Morris and Judith Browne Dianis; the three of us were contacted because of our research on Black girls increasingly being criminalized as early as kindergarten.[3] "Wild." "Disobedient." "Having attitude." These were words and phrases Dianis said she had encountered when people spoke of Black girls. Morris added "unladylike" and "displaying uncontrollable behavior" as examples from her own work. The first caller asked, "Is there a cultural element to this . . . ? Is it because you're an African American female? Does that mean you get to get away with these behaviors?" Dianis countered the caller by disrupting the idea that people are color-blind when they view behavior: "Disrespect is in the eye of the beholder. Insubordination is in the eye of the beholder." Dianis was pointing out that the behaviors of Black girls are viewed through different lenses, even when White students display similar behaviors.

Such lenses and associated perceptions impact the ways educators construct Black children. In my ethnography of formerly incarcerated Black girls who participated in a playwriting and performance workshop, I describe learning that these girls—student artists—used theater to define and redefine themselves to those who labeled them "delinquents," "troublemakers," "promiscuous," and "at-risk."[4] Through their theater work, these student artists embraced new ways to talk about themselves as "playwrights," "writers," "actors," and "artists" in order to shift the way others viewed them and how they viewed themselves. Essentially, these girls and the people around them had to engage in paradigm shifting to move past monolithic labels and stereotypes that held them captive in ways that undermined their ability to imagine their futures.

Beyond requiring a new way of communicating with others, paradigm shifting requires a new language to signal a new way of being in relationship with others. Leaving Chicago, where schools and communities were under-resourced, and where Black Americans struggled to be viewed as valued citizens, the African Hebrew Israelites of Jerusalem "saints" recreated themselves in just such a manner in the late 1960s, beginning with transformative language practices to reclaim their identity and uplift their community. Anthropologist John L. Jackson marveled that with these new language practices, "nothing is off limits or unworthy of close reading and rereading. It is all-encompassing, an elaborate new dictionary for an old and corrupted language."[5] I find that restorative justice work makes it possible for students and educators to exercise the "power to define" (to borrow from Jackson) and reclaim language in self-determined ways that reflect shared values.

The power to define is central to the work of restorative justice in education. In my view, one of the major thrusts of RJ work in education is to give children and youth, along with their families, teachers, staff, and administrators, the power to define themselves beyond static conceptions of race, class, gender, and ability as well as other labels and categories that capture neither the full humanity of a student ("eligible for free and reduced lunch," "English language learner," "boy," "girl," "undocumented," "trouble-maker," "college-bound," etc.) nor the nuances of that student's racial, ethnic, or cultural composition ("Asian/Pacific Islander," "Hispanic," "Black/African American," "White," etc.). Educators also need opportunities to define themselves, their roles, and how they view their work. School communities must engage in the exercise of reevaluating language practices—especially those tied to race, ethnicity, citizenship, and belonging. Therefore, I assert that the RJ paradigm is an invitation to develop "critical vocabularies,"[6] or what I refer to as "restorative justice discourses," that allow participants to capitalize on their individual and shared histories in order to construct more accurate portrayals of who they are and their positionality in the world using grammatical agency.[7]

The purpose of this chapter is to offer a conceptual framework for restorative justice in education. To support the paradigm-shifting work involved in establishing restorative justice in school contexts, I propose that RJ discourses and practices be grounded in four complementary pedagogical stances: (1) History Matters, (2) Race Matters, (3) Justice Matters, and (4) Language Matters. These pedagogical tools for creating and sustaining the restorative justice mind-set support a paradigm shift by enabling, for example, an RJ circle to become a site for boundary-crossing social engagement or an opportunity for stakeholders to achieve freedom and justice through the practice of defining and redefining themselves and those around them. Because these four pedagogical stances have overlapping aims and shared goals, this conceptual framework is best visualized as four nested circles (see figure 2.1).

PARADIGM-SHIFTING PEDAGOGICAL TOOLS

Two patterns strike me among educators who claim that restorative justice "isn't working": (1) they have not been trained in restorative justice, and (2) they have not engaged in the mind-set work that must occur for practitioners to be open to and fully immersed in restorative justice practice. For educators, such a mind-set shift requires complementary pedagogical stances that are consistent with the tenets and goals of restorative justice, which asks that each one of us recognize and affirm the importance and interconnectedness of history, race, justice, and language when we work through problems and solutions.

Pedagogical Stance 1: History Matters

The first pedagogical stance, History Matters, is the outermost circle in figure 2.1, representing the infinite journey of all educators to learn about the historical contexts that affect the schools and communities in which we teach. This stance requires that educators seek

FIGURE 2.1 *Four pedagogical stances for engaging in restorative justice work in education*

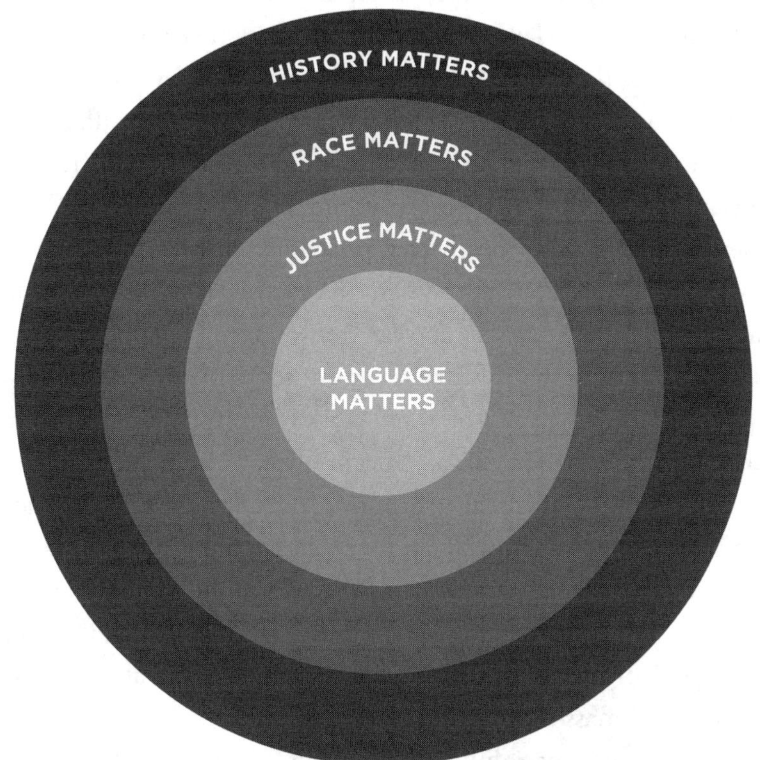

out histories that make us uncomfortable and force us to look critically at the group-level power dynamics that characterize our schools and communities. For example, approximately one year before the world witnessed the encounter between Shakara and Officer Fields, the school district that houses Spring Valley High, Richland County Two, simmered with racial tensions that prompted Black parents to form a Black Parents Association to address local concerns. I believe educators in this district should learn about how local history is inextricably linked to both race and local power dynamics, using multiple sources, including the families of the children they serve.[8] Such a learning process might allow educators in this district to reimagine their community, and themselves, in new ways.

In 2015, when I was on faculty at the University of Wisconsin–Madison, the campus selected Bryan Stevenson's *Just Mercy* as required reading to build community among students, staff, and faculty.[9] In this book, the author, who is the founder and director of the Equal Justice Initiative in Montgomery, Alabama, details his experiences representing death row prisoners who were either innocent or unfairly sentenced. When Stevenson visited Madison and other campuses that academic year, he was asked what was next for his work. Arguing that history is central to justice work, Stevenson responded that his equity-oriented work is grounded in a truth that should be a call to action for all citizens of the United States: "We are all carrying this illness, this disruption that has created a narrative of racial indifference, and because of that we continue to suffer . . . Slavery has not ended, it's evolved."[10] To continue to pursue justice, Stevenson and his colleagues believed they must confront this country's history of racial injustice, including slavery, "racial terror," segregation, and mass incarceration.

Many Americans think they know all they need to know about the enslavement of Africans in the Americas, but educators need and deserve time to learn and think about how the enslavement of Africans *continues* to impact all Americans and how this brutal history continues to play out through systemic racist policies, individual-level racism, and implicit bias. "Histories never leave us for another inaccessible place," asserts philosopher Angela Y. Davis. "They are part of us; they inhabit us and we inhabit them even when we are not aware of this relationship to history."[11] Restorative justice in the context of education is an opportunity to access these histories. History Matters, as a pedagogical stance, is an opportunity to access painful histories collectively and to address historical wrongdoing in education and in school communities.

Pedagogical Stance 2: Race Matters

Building on History Matters, the second pedagogical stance, Race Matters, is also informed by history and requires teachers to consider the role of racism and racist ideas in how they think about students as learners. What are our perceptions of learners based on their race and ethnicity? Why do we think this? Where do these ideas come from, and how can we replace them with more nuanced understandings of our students? What do our students and their families value and believe? In examining the social construction of race, racism, and racist lenses and ideas, we must consider the role of social movements seeking justice for Black, Latinx, and Indigenous children and their families in the context of the United States. The use of force against Shakara is connected to a history of racist ideas and propaganda that justified the enslavement of Africans in the Americas and rendered Black girls and women chattel, not feminine or worthy of careful handling or respectful treatment. To read the text of the footage of Shakara and Officer Fields, one would need to consider the role of race, racism, and racist lenses and ideas that perpetuate state-sanctioned violence against Black and Brown people in the United States.

Race Matters is thus a pedagogical stance that invites us to learn so that we might unlearn. The Equal Justice Initiative, as an example, began an organizational undertaking of historical research by creating an archive about lynching in America, because they believed it forced "more honest" conversations about race. Ignorance of such histories does not mean we do not carry the consequences of their impact.[12]

Using the stories of five individuals who have shaped the way people think and talk about race in the context of the United States, Ibram X. Kendi invites readers on a journey to shed racist ideas. Kendi's work is an ideal example of the power of this stance, because it underscores the fact that a commitment to thinking about why America is characterized by such profound racial inequality and tension tends to be a transformative journey of learning, self-reflection, and unlearning: "When you truly believe that the racial groups are equal, then you also believe that racial disparities must be the result of racial discrimination. Committed to this antiracist idea of group equality, I was able to self-critique, discover, and shed the racist ideas I had consumed over my lifetime while I uncovered and exposed the racist ideas that others have produced over the lifetime of America."[13]

Educational research continues to grapple with history and race in America's schools and to revisit the historical *Brown v. Board of Education* ruling. However, education historian Vanessa Siddle Walker reminds us that this ruling is not the beginning of the narrative. Walker troubles the standard narrative of segregated schools as inferior through an example of Black teachers in a segregated school in the South that encouraged its Black students to reach "their highest potential" using a discourse of love, care, and expectations.[14] These hidden stories of what Black teachers were able to do for Black children in decaying school buildings with weathered teaching materials keep us from knowing the pedagogical stances and strategies that Black teachers have used to create communities of eager learners, against the odds.[15] Various histories that contextualize current inequalities and injustices through the stories, struggles, and resilience of various racial groups should be shared in formal learning environments. A first step in doing so is tackling research related to the history of one's own school and surrounding communities.

Pedagogical Stance 3: Justice Matters

The third circle and pedagogical stance, Justice Matters, brings to the forefront social movements that dare to imagine a world where everyone—irrespective of race, ethnicity, socioeconomic status, gender, sexuality, or ability—is able to live with dignity and is recognized as belonging. This pedagogical stance is guided by a moral compass insisting we do right by people, a responsibility that is especially crucial for those entrusted with the lives of the children and youth in our classroom and school communities. Again, how Officer Fields responded to Shakara was *lawful*, in the sense of being protected by the state Disturbing Schools code; however, it was not *just* or ethical.

The more I spend time with teachers, both preservice and inservice, the more convinced I am that the word "justice" must remain a part of the restorative work. The omission of "justice" for the safer term "practices" undermines the potential to get educators to consider how racist ideas permeate the education system in both implicit and explicit ways. Justice Matters signals a need to grapple with history and engage in what needs to be done so that all children and their families receive justice in the form of access to high-quality teaching and learning opportunities.

One argument I hear from educators who resist the word "justice" is that they do not want anything linked to jails and prisons to become part of their work in schools. This is understandable, considering that schools serving Black, Latinx, and Indigenous children already tend to rely on surveillance and isolation to control students.[16] However, this reasoning also demonstrates how a criminal justice system culture permeates American culture; the word "justice" should not be interchangeable with the criminal justice system. In a lecture titled "Justice . . . Just Justice!" Gloria Ladson-Billings points out that the word "justice" has been compromised in myriad ways in educational contexts; she further posits that "social justice"—a widely used term in education—is not "expansive enough to help us confront the tremendous injustice that has a deafening grip on our society and keeps us so far away from everything we know as right and fair and just."[17]

The pedagogical stance Justice Matters acknowledges a more expansive justice that seeks to cultivate a generation of children who are free: free from labels that do not reflect their full humanity, free from categories that disrupt teachers' ability to engage with some of them, free from the threat of punishment in places of learning, and free to be confident learners. History, race, and justice matter when preparing children to be free. These pedagogical stances allow us to think about how racism and the violence of racism—both physical and symbolic—affect young lives. Davis argues that because people are not engaging in difficult conversations about race and racism, the persistence of racism has resulted in "the rearing of generations of Black people who have not learned how to imagine the future—who are not now in possession of the education and the imagination that allows them to envision the future."[18] When I visualize Justice Matters encircled by Race Matters and History Matters, I think about what it means to educate children for freedom. Not merely individual freedoms that produce more "silos," or successful individuals, but a "collective freedom" that allows and encourages children and educators to learn to be in positive relationship with each other.

Restorative justice, then, is a movement toward "collective freedom," which Robin D. G. Kelley argues is "more expansive and radical" than the freedoms that scholars like myself have argued come with being critically literate or being able to read, write, think, interrogate, and grapple with texts.[19] While I continue to believe that the ability to be agentive in literate practices is critical for youth, as evidenced by my ethnographic work with student poets from the Bronx who participated in the Power Writers class,[20] as well as student artists in the Girl Time program who penned plays about their lived experiences before, during, and after incarceration, I also learned that children and youth need so much more, including high-quality education, housing, and the ability to live the lives they desire and deserve.[21] Educators and schools can do some of this work using these pedagogical stances and engaging students in peacemaking/-keeping/-building circle processes, though they cannot do it all.

Pedagogical Stance 4: Language Matters

The fourth and final pedagogical stance, Language Matters, is the heart of these nested circles, providing tangible tools for addressing the complex work of reconciling history, race, and justice. Being mindful about how one uses language to speak to and about children—especially children from historically marginalized communities—is foundational to healthy relationships and should never be undermined.[22]

A justice-seeking movement in schools insists that no children are throwaways. Talking about our students marks an ideal place to begin this work. Challenging educators to refuse labels such as "troublemaker," Carla Shalaby shares the stories of students who were marked with this label in their schools and the impact such labels have on all of us. Shalaby writes, "We pay dearly for our failure to teach freedom, for our refusal to insist on being fully human."[23] We see this in the over-policing of children in schools like Spring Valley High, and we are also seeing justice and freedom interrupted for "undocumented" children, youth, and their families.

Educators—adults who interact with children on their way to school (e.g., bus drivers, crossing guards), in school (e.g., teachers, registrars, social workers, janitors, hall monitors, librarians, secretaries, administrators, school resource officers, counselors, volunteers), and after school (e.g., coaches, class and club sponsors)--can use language to build or even dismantle potential futures. The role of language was not an original objective when Zehr began his work to reframe crime and justice. "What I did not understand," Zehr said later, "was the extent to which our frames or assumptions are embedded in, and shaped by language and metaphor."[24]

Labeling students creates a deficit framing of children and youth in schools that is difficult to shed. Ladson-Billings offered one of the most compelling challenges to the language of schools and education by addressing what is often referred to as the "achievement gap," arguing that what America really has is an "education debt" that is owed to generations of Indigenous, Black/African American, and Latinx children and youth in American public schools. The concept of an education debt shifted the conversation of and responsibility for the so-called gap by pointing to the historic, moral, and economic debts owed to people and communities of color. At the core of America's understanding of who is deserving and worthy of a rigorous teaching and learning experience, or who has a right to education, are notions of citizenship and belonging. In earlier work, Ladson-Billings posited that education and literacy are historically linked to how America conceptualizes belonging and citizenship.[25] Classrooms and schools often reflect what has been referred to as a two-tiered system of citizenship:

> As we all know, the term "civil rights" refers to the rights of citizens, of all citizens, but because the very nature of citizenship in the United States has always been troubled by the refusal to grant citizenship to subordinate groups—indigenous people, African slaves, women of all racial and economic backgrounds—we tend to think of some people as model citizens, as archetypical citizens, those whose civil rights are never placed in question, the quintessential citizens, and others as having to wage struggles for the right to be regarded as citizens. And some—undocumented immigrants or "suspected" undocumented immigrants, along with ex-felons or "suspected" ex-felons—are beyond the reach of citizenship altogether.[26]

The very notion of citizenship is also part of America's tenuous relationship with race and racism. Who belongs? Who doesn't? Who looks the part? Who sounds and behaves the part? At best, restorative justice should seek to exchange what Davis refers to as "historically obsolete vocabularies" about race for "critical vocabularies" that can support restorative justice work in schools by creating opportunities for healthy relationships and bolstering activities designed undermine racism. Restorative justice offers words, concepts, and language that constitute "critical vocabularies," or what I refer to as "restorative justice discourses," that provide ways to talk with and about children while acknowledging their humanity.

Restorative justice discourse disrupts retributive mind-sets and processes in order to help participants discover new ways of talking about what Howard Zehr identifies as the three pillars of restorative justice: harms, needs, and obligations (described in the introduction).[27] I often use the example that an adult might ask a child to stop running if the environment has obstacles where the child can potentially get hurt. If the child continues to run and gets hurt, the first response might sound like "Didn't I tell you to stop running?" as opposed to "Are you okay? Can I help? What do you need?" The former implies that the priority is recognition that the child is at fault for the injury because the parent told him or her not to run, whereas the latter deliberately uses language to acknowledge the injury rather than situating blame or fault. In this vein, youth engagement expert Shawn Ginwright notes that, unlike *closed* words (e.g., resist, defend, disrupt, demand, fight, struggle, confront, destroy), *open* words (e.g., reimagine, dream, discover, create, design, imagine, play, invent) help educators prepare for the work ahead.[28]

Some within the RJ community challenge the word "restorative" in restorative justice. Elsewhere I ask, "Who is worthy of restoration? Who gets to determine this, and who or what are we restoring?"[29] Zehr, acknowledging the complexities of "re" words, offers the alternative to "transformative justice": "Those who advocate transformative justice also point out, with justification, that if restorative justice replicates the legal system's emphasis on individuals and does not address the larger, often structural, causes of offending and victimization, it will continue to perpetuate crime. They argue, then, for a transformative approach to justice that not only addresses individual wrongdoing but addresses the harms and obligations inherent in social, economic, and political systems."[30] Although this book uses the more common "restorative justice," I share the feeling that restorative justice practitioners must address individual wrongdoing and take steps to actively disrupt systemic injustice and wrongdoing.

WHY CIRCLES?

As students, teachers, and school staff engage in restorative justice circle processes, they develop sociocritical literacies—that is, they learn how to use their histories as resources for the present and the future.[31] In an RJ circle process, each participant listens and then has a chance to speak when it is their turn to hold the talking piece, which moves in one direction around the circle.[32] The facilitator initiates the conversation by posing a question or prompt, or presenting relevant artifacts, and then guiding participants, in turn, to provide context, exchange histories, define themselves, and name their actions, thus creating inclusive opportunities for participants to be agentive in building or repairing community in hopes of preempting harm (see figure 2.2). A "restorying" process often occurs whereby participants name and define themselves in ways that tend to be unknown or invisible to others. I always begin my circles with "Who are you and why are you here?" Simple questions can begin a process in which people have both the power to define and declare their identities and the opportunity to link their identity to their history or their future. An RJ circle might thus open with "What is the story of your name?" or "What is the story of your middle name?" It is during this restorying process that people begin

FIGURE 2.2 *Restorative justice circles as boundary-crossing social networks*

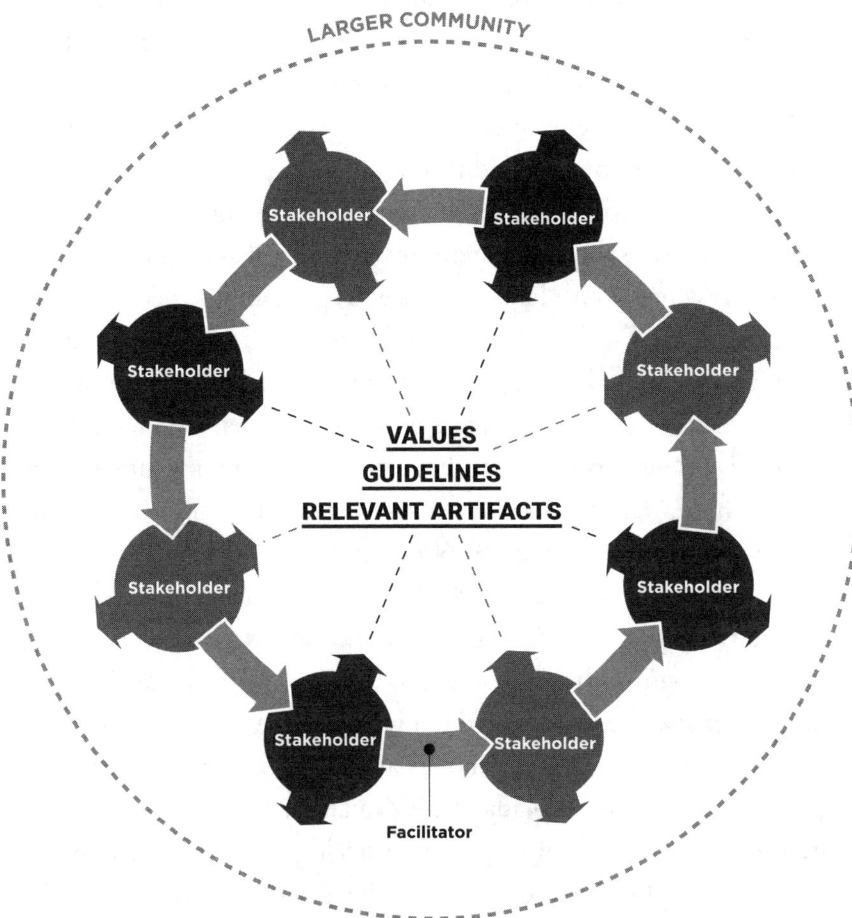

Figure 2.2 shows how RJ circles provide participants with opportunities to talk and listen using a talking piece that moves in one direction. Participants' individual and collective stories are shared within the circle while the wisdom/lessons are carried outside of the circle. Participants are anchored by a shared set of values and guidelines that they have determined together placed on the centerpiece inside the circle. These values and guidelines can be revisited throughout the process.

to form boundary-crossing social connections and circles become transformative learning spaces. Circle participants are anchored by a shared set of values and guidelines that they have determined together, which (as described in the introduction) are written down and placed on the centerpiece inside the circle, where they remain accessible and can be revisited throughout the process.

Borrowing from colleagues in psychology and social work, restorative justice circles can be theoretically understood as complex activity systems in which youth have the space to speak and be heard—often for the first time—while defining and contextualizing their lived experiences in a larger landscape of identity and history. Michael White argues that this type of narrative approach to identity or meaning making is essential because our lives are "shaped" by meaning, life is "multistoried," "storylines" are central to meaning making, and individuals (and communities) too often render their strengths invisible to themselves.[33] Figure 2.2 shows how the lessons and wisdom that emerge from participants' individual and collective stories are not only shared within the circle but also flow out from the circle when participant stakeholders share them within the larger community.

Circle processes, which scholars argue arose in Indigenous communities throughout Canada, New Zealand, and the United States, are often used as a tool to promote healthy dialogue, discussion, and understanding. In fact, in places like New Zealand and Northern Ireland, restorative justice processes—including circle processes and case conferencing—are *required* when youth offend.[34] The circle processes employed by Indigenous and Aboriginal people as an alternative to traditional criminal justice sentencing practices are being explored in school contexts.[35] It is important to underscore that circles, peacemaking circles in particular, "are not a neutral, value-free process."[36] As mentioned, stakeholders in the circle determine a set of shared values *before* topics and ideas are explored. Questions from the moderator or facilitator serve as mediating tools for narrative responses that help adolescents to contextualize their actions against a larger backdrop of lived and shared experiences.

It may be possible that restorative justice circle processes can begin to address social inequality by giving students and teachers in public schools a tool that disrupts polarizing discourses about who is and is not worthy of citizenship and, by extension, quality education. Racial disparities in school discipline have far-reaching implications across these domains. In 2012, in the first Senate hearing addressing the school-to-prison pipeline, the acting administrator of the US Department of Justice Office of Juvenile Justice and Delinquency Prevention (OJJDP), Melodee Hanes, testified about the overuse of court referrals in school discipline policies. According to Hanes, who cited two decades of research with OJJDP, the minute children set foot "in the juvenile justice system, their chances of becoming an adult offender go up 50 percent . . . Their chances of completing their education, their chances of getting a good job, their chances in life in general diminish significantly."[37] US public school students who are consistently punished for ambiguous reasons will find it difficult, if not impossible, to achieve the kind of academic success that gives them an opportunity in the aforementioned domains. Elsewhere I argue that restorative justice—when used properly by trained and skillful practitioners in schools—can begin to create, build, and sustain relationships that disrupt the two-tiered system of citizenship that exacerbates the "education debt" owed to American children.[38] Adam Gamoran argues that schooling cannot instill shared values throughout the US population if some youth do not have access to quality educational experiences.[39] Therefore, it is imperative that we continue to examine how schools can create "social networks that cross the boundaries of families, communities, and background . . . [that] help knit the fabric of American society."[40] Restorative justice circles, then, are pedagogical tools for school communities to restore, or in many cases transform, the "fabric" of an American society and democracy.

There have been times when I mention arranging chairs in a circle and people begin to roll their eyes and sigh deeply. I have even heard people making jokes that circles make them feel as if they are in Alcoholics Anonymous or group therapy. During one training facilitated by Rita Alfred from the Restorative Justice Training Institute, Alfred kindly responded to a participant who compared restorative justice circles to therapy, "No. Therapy is new. RJ is old." I recall a tense time when I was teaching tenth-grade English and my students were struggling to respect one another. Like many teachers, I was a roving teacher who did not have my own classroom and was thus at the whim of the teacher who had ownership of the classroom I was using. I often inherited classrooms with rows of desks, an arrangement that conflicts with my teaching philosophy and style. One classroom had rows of desks on both sides of the classroom, so students on one side of the room faced another group of students on the other side of the room. It was as if this physical setup encouraged the two groups of students to interact as if they were playing for competing teams. One day, out of exasperation (it certainly was not out of wisdom at that point), I asked my students to "circle up." This request felt intuitive, though I had seen that proximity sometimes helped when students were lashing out at each other. One of my students moaned, "Ms. Fisher, I feel naked. We're too close." Indeed, we *were* close, and closeness sometimes makes it more difficult to lash out at others. The entire class, including that student, started to laugh, and we agreed that, despite the initial discomfort, something changed when we were in a circle. I sat in the circle with my students, and we read and wrote together for the entire period. The teasing stopped, and it felt good—until my senior colleague who "owned" the room came in and expressed her annoyance that we had moved her precious desks. Her opposition and glares continued, but we "circled up" about once a week after that, or whenever things felt a little unstable. (Of course, we always put the desks back the way they were when we entered the room.)

It can take some time to feel comfortable using restorative justice circles. I have trained with teachers across disciplines who wanted to do the work and take it back to their schools. However, many were worried that their colleagues would think sitting in a circle was too ephemeral. Others knew that many of their colleagues would not want to sit at the same level as the students, because they like to maintain "authority." Circles take practice, and one of the most important aspects of the circle is introducing a new way of looking at old words and including objects—a talking piece, a centerpiece, values, and guidelines co-created by circle participants or stakeholders. Words such as "respect" and "confidentiality" are defined and redefined to meet the needs of the stakeholders in the circle. With the guidance of a facilitator, circle participants are led through a series of activities and questions that begin to unpack *who* they are and *why* they are in that specific space in that particular moment. The talking piece is a symbolic reminder that there is a time to talk and, perhaps more important, a time to listen. Circles can be fluid in that they are created to fit the needs of the stakeholders and thus provide opportunities for what Kelley refers to as "collective striving for real democracy."[41] Restorative justice circles have the potential to be "change labs" where people are transformed through a participatory process that provides opportunities for them to learn more about the lives of others they have previously disregarded or even held in contempt.[42]

SUMMARY

As an equity-oriented scholar, I draw from cultural-historical activity theory (CHAT) to reimagine the work of restorative justice circles in schools. CHAT scholarship begins with the understanding that children are born with "profound equality" as opposed to "fixed differential potentials."[43] CHAT seeks to understand not only human behavior and interaction in activity systems in the present but also how participants bring their historicized selves to these activities. With cultural practice as the unit of analysis, CHAT invites inquiry that prioritizes "issues of race, culture, and learning" or how "hierarchies of power" in society are often "reproduced in the local activities of the classroom."[44] CHAT insists on participants working together toward the goal of solving problems and offering new vocabularies as opposed to being "timid" and complacent.[45]

Restorative justice circles are transformative learning communities offering unique opportunities to practice freedom, justice, and democratic engagement that transform participants' ways of engaging and relating to other participant stakeholders. There are many activity systems at work in schools. This book focuses on the cultural practices of classroom and school communities, how teachers and adults in a school building understand and enact their roles, and how shifting those ideas and practices might build a more inclusive and engaged community of learners. Stakeholders use storytelling to build relationships and consensus about how to meet these needs. Restorative justice practitioner and theorist Kay Pranis contends that in addition to being "the most fundamental way to practice democracy," restorative justice requires participants "to look at our own role in harmful behavior, and to recognize harm to anyone is harm to us as well."[46] This practice could help classroom and school communities begin looking within and focus on developing tools rather than pathologizing students, their families, and communities.

The four pedagogical stances and the RJ circle process described in this chapter are all ways to begin the work of disrupting inequities and dismantling racial and other injustices; they also orient us to what might replace the boundaries and barriers associated with hurtful histories, policies, practices, and labels. In chapter 3 I relate the story of a Midwestern high school that chose to begin restorative justice work by training its students to be RJ circle keepers.

CHAPTER 3

"WE LIVE IN A NATION OF FREEDOM"

Learning with Students

As on so many mornings when I was a participant observer at Kennedy High School during the 2014–2015 academic year, I stopped to listen when an administrator read the announcements over the loudspeaker. These were always followed by the Pledge of Allegiance, which brought me back to my own days as a student, standing with my right hand over my heart while reciting the words "with liberty and justice for all," a ritual without ceremony that felt more like a disruption to the flow of the morning than something worthy of my full attention. After all, no adult took time to explicate this script we had duly memorized, nor did we interrogate words such as "liberty" or "justice" as students—not the way I would eventually grapple with these concepts as a classroom teacher and later as a scholar. For some reason, on this day I resisted my natural inclination to tune out the words and heard the administrator offer a prelude to the pledge: "We live in a nation of freedom; therefore, participation in the Pledge of Allegiance is voluntary."

This startled me. Did the announcer always make this statement before the pledge? I asked several teachers and students in the building if this was new. They assured me that the same statement was made every day. Having spent so much time in schools that were focused on controlling the minds, bodies, and voices of children and youth—especially those who were Black, Latinx, and Indigenous—I marveled that a school community would invite students to be autonomous with regard to their participation in saying the pledge. I wondered if a school community could create a culture that values student agency when it comes to democratic engagement, justice, and citizenship. I also wondered what role, if any, language might play in the culture of such school communities. Is it possible for schools to shift from zero-tolerance or punitive discourses to restorative justice discourses, and can such a shift expand a school's capacity for practicing justice? What would a discourse of restoration and transformation look and sound like in schools? What are students saying, thinking, and doing about justice, and how are youth theorizing what it means to practice justice?

My work in the Southeast, Northeast, and, more recently, on the West Coast, assures me that these are appropriate questions in many US cities and regions.[1] While a Midwestern city in Wisconsin, the site of this school community, may not resonate as a likely place for addressing inequalities in education, the Annie E. Casey Foundation's "Race to Results" report ranked Wisconsin the worst state (fiftieth) in which to raise African American children.[2] Before my family moved to Madison, Wisconsin, everyone we spoke with talked about the city being a great place to raise a family. We were told the public schools were strong and the neighborhood where we purchased a home would give us access to the best schools. However, middle-class Black families who lived in Madison shared a much different narrative. Black parents who were involved and invested in the many ways schools ask us to be found their children being viewed and treated as if they were incapable—and their perspective as parents disregarded.

After settling into my new city, I learned about the Disproportionate Minority Contact (DMC) working group. A multiethnic coalition of judges, lawyers, law enforcement professionals, social service workers, educators, juvenile justice workers, and youth-serving nonprofit organizations, the DMC group seeks to reduce how frequently Black and Latinx people come into contact with law enforcement. Colleagues in this group were candid and admitted that the number of youth entering the juvenile justice system in Madison would decrease drastically if schools ceased requesting law enforcement support for incidents they could address themselves. As the mother of Black children, my impetus for joining this group had less to do with scholarship and more to do with personal concerns about racial injustice in policing and the criminalization of Black and Brown children. In light of bleak statistics demonstrating vast racial disparities in Dane County, which houses Madison,[3] I found it compelling that so many people were deeply committed to reducing and eliminating these disparities at the local level. I also learned that one of the school districts in Dane County was attempting to incorporate a sustainable restorative justice culture in its schools. To this end, the district formed a unique partnership with TRANSFORM,[4] a nonprofit organization that provides technical assistance for implementing restorative justice in schools. TRANSFORM did this by training students as RJ circle process facilitators or "circle keepers." Kennedy High School was one of the first to adopt this model. Student circle keepers, or SCKs, were invited by administrators and teachers to facilitate restorative justice circles that were focused primarily on conflicts between students or between students and teachers.

The purpose of this chapter is to highlight how SCKs at Kennedy conceptualize *justice* and *restorative justice*, as well as how they view the work and importance of restorative justice. While many RJ practitioners argue that schools should focus on training staff, teachers, and administrators because these professionals should be held accountable for building school community, the voices and actions of SCKs at Kennedy suggest that accountability and school culture can—and should—also be student opportunities. I purposefully begin with student perspectives rather than stories of the experiences of educators at Kennedy, because we rarely have the opportunity to learn from students first. These SCKs are knowledgeable and experienced RJ practitioners in their school, and this chapter provides insight into how they view relationships and discipline in school. In my study at Kennedy, I saw how training students in restorative justice fostered agency and ownership over the paradigm and processes previously in use. Interview data suggest that students think about discipline in nuanced ways and have keen observations about school practices. Ultimately, SCKs took their restorative justice work seriously and believed it encouraged healthy relationships in their school community. After describing the methodology of this study, I share the perspectives these student circle keepers shared with me during focus group and individual meetings.

CONTEXT

My case study took place during the 2013–2014 and 2014–2015 school years, after I had already spent two academic years getting to know students by attending school-wide assemblies that showcased student talent, attending leadership trainings for students, and talking to staff about their restorative justice work. During this preparatory phase, Kennedy's student community coordinator, "Mrs. Luz," the administrator who worked most closely with the student circle keepers, helped me identify five staff members who were deeply involved in Kennedy's restorative justice work. Mrs. Luz gathered school community nominations of such staff and collaborated with a colleague who was part of the initial RJ training to confirm that the nominees were appropriate for the purposes of this study. Findings related to my interviews with staff, particularly regarding how RJ training and implementation has influenced the way these educators talk about and approach their work, is described in chapter 4.

After all of the participants had been selected, Mrs. Luz helped me organize a lunch period focus group on May 1, 2014. Every one of the thirteen SCK students invited to the focus group attended, thanks to pizza and Mrs. Luz's encouragement. One student told me that if Mrs. Luz called, these students answered. It was evident she enjoyed being with students, and they, in return, enjoyed being with her. Of the thirteen SCKs who participated in the focus group, I subsequently interviewed eleven.[5] All participants were seniors who Mrs. Luz felt had plenty of institutional memory and the most experience with facilitating circles. SCKs at Kennedy were not merely the "usual suspects," that cohort of people who tend to be conspicuously active in secondary schools; some had been chosen because they had experienced strained relationships with adults in the building at some point in their high school career. The group was a mix of students with solid grades who were college-bound and active in other groups on campus, as well as students who had not been active in any extracurricular activities prior to their restorative justice work.

Before conducting the interviews, I spent time looking at TRANSFORM's materials and participated in one of their trainings. TRANSFORM was forthcoming about its larger agenda—dismantling racism—and their restorative justice work was unapologetically designed as a racial justice agenda. Therefore, student circle keepers learned about racial disparities between Black and White families in Dane County and reviewed data confirming that Black and Latinx students experience suspension more than their White and Asian peers. TRANSFORM talked about race and racism, including institutional racism. While the organization's work focused on training students, its members also trained educators and held community trainings that were specific to local contexts.

TRANSFORM wanted to make circle processes accessible to all, so Kennedy adopted certain protocols. For example, circles at Kennedy opened with stakeholders reading and responding to inspirational quotes by famous people. Student circle keepers chose from a set of quotes on laminated cards held together by a binder ring. Having a prop like this on hand made it easier to transition into a community-building exercise in the first round. Because SCKs were often helping to repair "harm circles," circle processes that took place after conflicts occurred, their members had to be prepared. As an RJ circle facilitator and trainer, I know that preparation can take a lot of time and thought. I appreciated how Kennedy used "props" to ensure that SCKs could not make the excuse that they were not prepared for a circle. SCKs also had access to a set of laminated blue paper circles with values written on them (e.g., "non-judgment," "inclusion," "respect," "responsibility," "honesty"), as well as a set of laminated green paper circles with guidelines written on them (e.g., "respect the talking piece," "confidentiality," "listen with an open mind," "phones/electronics away"). I know many practitioners shudder at the thought of a premade set of values and guidelines, as working together to establish such a framework is an important part of the RJ circle process (see chapter 2); however, stakeholders in schools always struggle for time, and Kennedy was no exception. With TRANSFORM's support, the school attempted to minimize the number of excuses one could make for not serving as an SCK by making the process as smooth as possible. TRANSFORM also assigned a restorative justice practitioner (RJP) to support the work at schools. The RJP visited the campus at least twice a week. However, students and educators did not feel they could wait for these specific days to hold circles. What if there were a need for a circle on a Tuesday and the RJP was not scheduled until Thursday or Friday? Trained student circle keepers thus offered more flexibility for Kennedy and seemed more sustainable.

In the remainder of this chapter, I emphasize how the student participants in this study communicated their understanding of restorative justice and the RJ circle processes practiced in their school. Five themes emerged; these student circle keepers said that the framework and tools of restorative justice are valuable because they allow students to (1) pursue equality; (2) problem-solve; (3) humanize Youth Court, a peer-led process to address wrongdoing using criminal court language and tools; (4) unlearn and relearn words; and (5) foster positive interactions outside the circle.

"EVERYBODY NEEDS TO HAVE THAT EQUALITY": WHY RJ MATTERS TO STUDENTS

I posed several questions to the SCK focus group, including "Who and what is restorative justice for?" I underscored that I did not have answers, telling them, "I am asking questions that I don't have answers for, because I'm trying to figure out the answers too." The first student to respond named a "power dynamic" in schools as a reason for restorative justice: "So a lot of times [there's] the power dynamic between students and teachers making [students] feel like they're less." Once this notion of a power dynamic entered the circle, the students built on the relationship between restorative justice and the need to temper this perceived power dynamic with at least one space where students could imagine their needs as being equally as important as the needs of the adults in the building. Students in the focus group argued that in restorative justice circles, teachers and students are on "equal ground":

> I kinda feel like, because restorative justice is a program that mends broken relationships; it's like when you come into a restorative justice circle, everybody kind of has equal ground. The teacher [is] not looked at as a teacher, and the student [is]

> not looked at as a student. Everybody needs to be respected, and everybody needs to have that equality. So the teacher can say how [he or she] feels without the student being too offended. The students can say how they feel without having that idea or threat and feeling that they might be suspended. The circle is the space where everybody is respected and everybody can share exactly how they feel and what they want to say. ("Jussie," May 1, 2014)

Students accepted that they could not expect to be or feel respected if fixed identities such as "teacher" and "student" remained in place. These real and imagined titles impeded relationships and opportunities for clear communication, goal setting, and establishing shared values. If these elements are not in place, the SCKs claimed, many students will not learn in these contexts. SCKs often referenced the words "equal" or "equality":

> [In circle] everybody gets an equal opportunity to say what they feel, their opinions and stuff. So that's the whole part of the talking piece. We share; whenever one person has the talking piece it's that person's turn to talk and everybody else is listening. So if you have something to say—and there's no judging or anything—so if you have something to say, then share it and then we'll all listen and then discuss, you know, about that. ("Derek," May 8, 2014)

For two student circle keepers, lessons about listening and establishing a sense of equality also came from an unexpected community nested within the larger Kennedy community. Derek and "Kerry" had taken American Sign Language (ASL) classes for four years at Kennedy and planned to continue their ASL studies in college. Kerry noted that the powerful listening practices and values in the ASL program were also reflected in the framework of her work as a restorative justice practitioner. She asserted that Kennedy's ASL teachers and students view each other as peers because effective inclusive communication is their sole priority: "In each ASL class, [teachers] circle you up because you have to always be able to see each other—and signing, it's all visual, so it helps to be in that circle, and we're not allowed to really sit behind a person."

Because of the physical space and the awkward shape of the classroom, it was impossible to have a full circle in the classroom housing ASL. However, the teachers improvised and created half circles, which, Kerry said, "still leaves the teacher to see all the students, and there is no hiding behind another student":

> Everyone is seen. Everyone is heard . . . because they're [seen]. As soon as you start signing, people are turned around and looking and paying attention. At all times, there's a signer who sits in the back of the room but still part of the circle, so everyone can turn and look at her, and that's in every single class. They even do it in college. They'll no longer use the desks like that. They'll even stand up in a circle for sign language, because they want everyone to be equal. So that's why when we're in the circle we want everyone to feel as if they're equal, so we talk about equality, things like that. Even though there are adults in the room, you're able to view that adult as your peer. (May 8, 2014)

Kerry dared to imagine life beyond Kennedy by looking forward to ASL classrooms in college, where she figured desks and other obstructions and hierarchies would not be an issue. Derek made similar comparisons to the ASL program, and other SCKs in the focus group underscored notions of equality as they attempted to capture the role of restorative justice in their school community:[6]

> That's really what restorative justice is to me . . . It's a community and it helps to bring us together, and . . . it's where everybody's equal, and sometimes we don't feel as everybody's equal here. Especially while we're in the circle, we always say that everybody's equal . . . 'cause it's really hard if you're in a conflict or you're having a trouble with a teacher, and you always feel like the teacher is gonna win the argument because they're upper. They're upper in the standards 'cause they're a teacher. I mean they're older and they know better. But we always tell them in the circle that everybody's equal, and that really helps most of the kids talk it out and figure stuff out, because they don't always feel like they can accomplish anything 'cause of the teachers' being above. ("Jennifer," June 5, 2014)

This notion that teachers would always "win" in conflicts with students seemed reasonable to Jennifer because "they're older and they know better." Though the students' words showed that restorative justice circles create a sense of equality in that moment, it was not clear that students felt that the moment and associated sense of equality always carried over into the other spaces they occupied with their teachers. Because I did not wish to push student circle keepers to talk about this in the focus group, I returned to some of these ideas in the individual interviews.

"A JIGSAW PUZZLE THAT YOU JUST HAVE TO FIGURE OUT:" HOW STUDENTS DEFINE RJ

In my ethnography of student poets, *Writing in Rhythm: Spoken Word Poetry in Urban Classrooms*,[7] I discuss the power of asking students to define various words, phrases, and concepts used in their classrooms and school communities. Establishing definitions may seem like a mundane beginning, but they help us gain a more nuanced understanding of the impact of discourses on students' lives and how students make sense of the discourses used by educators. In the context of Kennedy High School, I wanted to understand how members of this school community conceptualized justice and restorative justice that could contribute to a restorative justice discourse. Throughout my research, I have found that when adult facilitators and youth participants share a discourse that is central to their objectives, there are opportunities for expansive learning.[8]

All interviews began with my asking SCKs to tell me about who they were and what brought them to the work of restorative justice. In chapter 2 I discussed the importance of the "power to define" and how words can spur action. It is important to understand how learners interpret the words educators are using in order to see where meaning converges and diverges. My first request—asking student circle keepers to define "justice" and "restorative justice"—provoked passionate responses. As SCKs began to define justice, I noted their use of words such as "wrong," "the right way," and "getting something solved." One student even posited, "With [typical discipline] you feel like it's in print" ("Taraji," June 5, 2014). When defining "restorative justice," SCKs employed words like "building," "making," "lifting, "fixing," and "resolving," signaling that restorative justice is a process (as opposed to something static, or "in print") in which youth participants are civic actors held accountable for making/putting things right. In chapter 1 I described Viola's understanding of restorative justice as "justice on both sides" or "making it right in a way that both sides can come to an agreement," which highlights the perceived mismatch of students' and educators' objectives, positioning that often leads to conflicts. Such conflicts, according to SCKs at Kennedy, could be either avoided or resolved if everyone had an opportunity to be heard and to listen, to provide clarity and seek clarity, and to come together to share as civic actors entitled to the same rights. I understood the work of restorative justice at Kennedy to be a movement toward reclaiming the democratic aims of public schooling, and I understood SCKs as ambassadors of this work.

The SCKs facilitated various types of circles, but most of the circles were focused on conflict. Derek (self-identified as "African American" and "male") facilitated what he referred to as "conflict circles." According to Derek, the process forces students to question why they were upset in the first place: "We're building that relationship back together between the two people . . . just basically putting back together . . . I don't know how to say this—like making [pause]—just making the problem go away so you can just, like, drop it and be like, "Okay that was silly. You know there's no reason to be fighting over something like this. We can be friends" (May 8, 2014). There still seemed to be a binary in the way student circle keepers viewed this work as a conflict between two people, with little or no consideration of the expansive notion of stakeholders found in restorative justice theory. The pervasiveness of the binary perspective could be due to the types of circles these students experienced.

Student circle keepers at Kennedy often discussed justice and restorative justice together. For example, Jussie depicted justice as dealing with an individual who experienced harm or who had been "knocked down already" by using justice to "[put] them back on their two feet." Advocates for restorative justice argue that the US criminal justice system does not put people who experience harm "on their feet," as Jussie suggested. Victims often wait long periods of time for court hearings and trials and are not always kept abreast of how the case is unfolding. Many of their questions go unanswered. Jussie understood "justice" to be singular or victim-centered, whereas "restorative justice" took the community into consideration. Jussie elaborated about this idea of restorative justice striving for more balance among stakeholders:

> I think . . . there's kind of like two justices. [When] you're in court . . . it's more like forced, and then RJ is like everybody [is] doing it voluntarily. Because you can just sentence somebody to a suspension, to volunteer services, and hope that they get it. Hope that it clicks in their head. But restorative justice [means] you're gonna talk it out and we're not leaving until everybody understands what went wrong, or at least until everybody gets it off their chest in a safe place. (May 8, 2014)

Jussie, who also participated in the school's Youth Court program, found that typical discipline practices—suspending students or assigning them work detail on campus—left justice to chance and one could only "hope" that students would understand the impact of what they did, or that something "clicks in [their] head" that there are better ways to be in relationship with the school community. As a student circle keeper, Jussie experienced restorative justice as providing a tangible way to support someone who caused harm to think about his or her actions, and to talk through it with peers and those who may have been affected. RJ circles, then, attempt to answer everyone's questions and ensure that everyone understands the next steps. While Jussie described RJ circles as a "safe space," practitioners are starting to question this notion of safety as the field grows. Scholars have warned against the notion of safe spaces, especially in what may appear to be a homogenous community.[9] One can never guarantee or be guaranteed safety. School discipline policies and practices can also create a caste system that privileges students who understand the rules of engagement or who present themselves in ways that make those who represent the status quo (i.e., White, middle-class) feel comfortable.

I found that SCKs who defined themselves as Black/African American often held conservative perspectives about wrongdoing, which reminded me of respectability politics among people of color. In his critique of "the New Jim Crow," James Forman Jr. asserts that scholarship must address the fact that Blacks have called for more law enforcement in their own communities. Forman contends that mass incarceration is also an aspect of Black citizens demanding safety in their own communities.[10] Elsewhere I argue that people of color benefit from Blacks on the "outside" ("free") distancing themselves from Blacks on the "inside" ("incarcerated"), which is a shift from the widely held position during the Black Power movement that all prisoners of color were political prisoners.[11] As an example, before she began engaging in the work of restorative justice, Kerry's view of "justice" could be viewed as conservative, straightforward, and simple: you do something wrong, you go to jail:

> Before, I kinda thought [justice] was [if] you did something wrong, something wrong should be done to you. If you do something wrong you go to jail; I was really stuck on that. You do something wrong, that's what you should do; you should go to jail and you should have time to think about it, [and] that's the reason that you go to jail. But then I came here and started getting into restorative justice, and I started thinking there's a lot of things that's behind it. Not all people deserve to go to jail; some people do need counseling, but for certain crimes they always get sent there. Or a lot of times they get sent there and sometimes a little bit of counseling and connecting could probably fix whatever was damaged to make them do the crime. But since we don't have enough of that in the justice system, it will continue to be jail all the time. So that [perspective] is kind of changing [for me]. (May 8, 2014)

The beliefs that undergird Kerry's view of crime and punishment are embedded in notions of personal responsibility.[12] Kerry, like most Americans, was "stuck on that." However, the paradigm shift to restorative thinking requires that we consider context or, as Kerry offered, learning what is "behind" people's actions. Through circle keeping, which is by no means formal counseling, there is time and space for a "little bit of counseling," and, most importantly, "connecting." Kerry learned that the actions of those who caused harm should be addressed to support this person in being a full participant of the community in question. Interconnectedness is indeed a very compelling strand in restorative justice theory.[13] Kerry approached the RJ process as if it were a puzzle:

> I feel as if your problem is being restored. It's going from being a problem to just a situation. It's not as big. It's not holding you down. It's no longer a chip on your shoulder. It's just something in front of you—a jigsaw puzzle that you just have to figure out. And it helps the situation to know that it's not as bad as it really is; it's not as bad as you may think it is. And it helps you resolve it. And that's kind of the restorative [part of it]. (May 8, 2014)

If I were to frame one lesson from this study as central to the work of restorative justice, it would be inspired by Kerry's observations. How can educators transition to the view that what a student or something a student has done is a "situation" instead of a "problem"? In other words, how can education exchange the cycle of punishing children who are "problems" for a process that focuses on accountability and learning new tools and mind-sets that might improve future choices and outcomes? Kerry viewed justice, in the context of restorative justice practices, as a process of taking responsibility for situations and outcomes: "I feel like justice is getting something solved. For example, if a teacher and a student aren't getting along and the grade isn't going as well and the [student] is having trouble and they can't communicate with the teacher, [the student] would come in a circle and they would talk about it instead of not talking about it. [If] this [student is] getting a referral or something like that, they can talk about it and improve [the situation]" (May 8, 2014).

Kerry underscored how everyone involved in an incident or disruption is also responsible for co-creating an action plan to make things right. Here, Kerry began to unpack one of the themes I saw in conversations with student circle keepers. SCKs considered restorative justice circles to be the only space in schools where students could address teachers without fear of retaliation. In the context of these circles, students experienced a specific kind of freedom to address adults with a guaranteed opportunity to share how they experienced a situation or dynamic. There was mutual respect, as opposed to a culture where students are expected to show respect that they do not see reciprocated.

Another SCK, Taraji (self-identified as "African American" and "female"), described RJ circles as offering options to those involved: "But, basically, justice is just like everything going right, like the right way and what's supposed to be done. You feel like [typical discipline] is in print. Restorative justice is basically . . . letting [students] know all of their options and ways to solve situations and basically just, like, being honest and truthful in the circles, and I would describe it as something that helps students see another student's perspective" (June 5, 2014).

Taraji's reflections hint that perspectives and points of view are reread and resituated in a liberating way in the context of restorative justice in schools. Rather than having a student's actions being prejudged "in print," a student would have options. For example, when I think about Shakara at Spring Valley High School, so much attention was focused on the fact that she did not put away her cell phone when asked to do so. The cell phone became a distraction and a prop to justify the violent physical removal of a nonviolent child from the classroom setting. Shakara did not get an opportunity to define herself, name her own actions, or take accountability—and no one in the room got the opportunity to learn from collective problem-solving—because Shakara broke a rule within a static, top-down "justice" system that was "in print."

"YOUTH COURT IS FOR THE BIGGER STUFF:" YOUTH COURT IN A RESTORATIVE COMMUNITY

At the time of this study, Kennedy High School had not completely moved away from justice "in print," as evidenced by its Youth Court program, which was grounded in and depended on criminal justice discourse. One of the challenges in building and practicing a restorative justice discourse in schools is that such practices are often rolled out while the institution continues to use punitive discourse in other spaces and contexts. Having punitive systems in place, of course, makes some community members feel safer. Scholar and prison abolitionist Erica Meiners began to address this in her groundbreaking book *Right to Be Hostile: Schools, Prisons, and the Making of Public Enemies.*[14] When asked about her views of prison abolition, Meiners was often confronted with the question "But what are we going to do with the really bad people?" Meiners underscores that her stance as a prison abolitionist is unfaltering; therefore, instead of looking for the exceptions (who is "bad" enough to go to prison), she wants to learn more about how to address wrongdoing. If suspending children is a tool, it will be used. If expelling children is an option, it will be exercised. If calling armed police to remove a child from a classroom is part of a school's culture, it will occur. If jails for children and adults exist, particularly as for-profit businesses, they will be filled. These "ifs" all exist in the United States, begging the question "How can there truly be a paradigm shift toward restorative justice if these other mechanisms remain in place?"

Like many schools across the United States, Kennedy has a Youth Court program. According to Elise Jensen, Youth Courts "are typically peer-driving: teens serve as the judge, jury, bailiff, and advocates, though some models include an adult as the judge."[15] Youth Court at Kennedy seemed to function as insurance for RJ circle processes. It was viewed as more systematic and structured, with clear and concise steps to follow up with stakeholders. Prior to my research in communities practicing restorative justice, I was skeptical of Youth Court coexisting with restorative justice. I wondered how a community in the early phases of implementing restorative justice could be committed to the necessary change in mind-set with the language of Youth Court in the same building. I wanted to know which students were asked to "judge," how they were selected, and how that hierarchy and power dynamic among students impacted their perceptions of one another and shaped their relationships.

At Kennedy, Youth Court maintained a retributive discourse that included the words "court," "sentence," and "jury." In listening to and learning from student circle keepers, I discovered they did not find the relationship between restorative justice and Youth Court to be as dichotomous as I did. Several SCKs participated in both restorative justice and Youth Court and used the former to inform their decisions in the latter in order to make the Youth Court experience more restorative. SCKs valued their restorative justice training in the context of Youth Court, while acknowledging the differences:

> I believe that justice kind of falls in the line of Youth Court. It's not necessarily a punishment, but . . . it's basically a punishment, I believe. But it's not maximum punishment. It's not the most that you can punish. So I would say justice is basically just

> getting back what you put out there. I believe the biggest part of [restorative justice] is "restore," because instead of getting back what you deserve in a maybe negative way, if you put negativity out there, restoring kind of fills the emptiness of whatever you put out. So kind of restoring that punishment, instead of doing a punishment . . . doing a more intimate circle and realizing why you've done what you've done. (Kerry, May 8, 2014)

Somewhere between punishment and "not necessarily punishment," Youth Court, according to Kerry, was restorative and wasn't "the most one could punish." Restorative justice theory rejects the notion of "guilt" and the long-term impact of being "guilty." Viewing justice as a baseline for treating people fairly, Kerry thought of restorative justice as a mechanism to respond to an "emptiness" in people's lives. This was one of the many examples that confirmed that, through RJ circle processes, student circle keepers developed and practiced empathy with and for their peers and teachers.

Jussie (self-identified as "African American" and "male") asserted that restorative justice was not offered to all students. This point was at the core of my questions about the coexistence of RJ and Youth Court. Is restorative justice being practiced if schools get to select which students and scenarios are worthy of the process? To be sure, Kennedy reduced suspensions and expulsions when they began practicing restorative justice; however, predictable racial disparities persisted. Black students continued to be suspended at much higher rates than their non-Black peers, because a paradigmatic shift away from viewing Black children as disruptive had yet to occur. Jussie outlined the hierarchy of responses to wrongdoing at Kennedy. According to Jussie, Youth Court was reserved for incidents involving violence:

> The way I kind of look at it is restorative justice does a lot of, like, smaller stuff, and Youth Court is more like the bigger

> stuff. A lot of [Youth Court cases come] from different places. Fights. And, also, not everybody has the opportunity to explore those justice circles, and the only way you benefit from the circle is if the person wants to be in the circle. And then [Youth Court] is, like, our next best thing to try to help them out. And [Youth Court] is not the greatest, but I have—we will, like, sentence them to some kind of community service. I've even done it where kids just aren't connected to the school, so we sentence them to try new clubs or something like that. So it's just like, it's kind of . . . we get to ask them questions, kind of—that's really how we go about it. We ask them questions about how their life is and the overall sense of how the person is, and then it helps. (May 1, 2014)

For Jussie, the "restorative" aspect of his work in Youth Court was that a "sentence" might stipulate that the wrongdoer "try new clubs"—imposed community engagement. Jussie had come to believe that students who feel a sense of belonging are less likely to experience or initiate conflicts. Viola also talked about the need for students to get involved and become active members of the school community:

> And I feel like through Youth Court you put the person in the place where they feel uncomfortable, but I feel like it also takes that being uncomfortable to realize that you really did do something wrong and you can be getting a ticket, but we're giving you the opportunity to get it together. And at the same time, we're soft on them 'cause it's like "What are you good at?" "What do you want to be involved in?" "What extra push do you need?" So it's like you tap them on the hand because they did something wrong, but at the same time you're rubbing on their back to let them know you're there for them . . . We can

> help you get through whatever you're trying to get through. We can help you kind of move, take those steps to move forward that you might not have had and that might have led you to being sentenced to Youth Court. (June 4, 2014)

Like Jussie, Viola's work in Youth Court borrowed from her work as a student circle keeper even as she employed incarceration discourse. I started using the term "incarceration discourse" because most of the formerly incarcerated girls I interviewed could only focus on what they did "wrong" and then launch into a vague script about "doing better" or "making better choices."[16] It was difficult to determine what a better choice might look like, especially since most of the girls were returning to the same under-resourced schools (or sometimes worse if their original school refused to readmit them). I started asking future-oriented questions to children entangled in the juvenile justice system in order to get them to focus on their needs and what it would take to have those needs met.

Many students who went to Youth Court at Kennedy had received "tickets" for infractions like theft or other incidents that occurred off campus. Administrators decided who would go through a Youth Court process as an alternative to being referred to law enforcement: "Youth Court kinda gives you an ultimatum, something that you can do instead of getting a ticket. And Youth Court also will kind of make it as you've seen what you did wrong all the time. In restorative justice, it's not like thrown in your face that you did something wrong. It's '[SCKs] are a support system.' '[SCKs will] help you get through it.' [SCKs ask,] 'What happened prior to doing it? What led you to do it?' A 'do you need anyone to talk to?' kind of thing" ("Mary," May 8, 2014). Mary viewed Youth Court as conveying to students that their wrongdoing was calculated. According to Mary, Youth Court gave a more permanent "ultimatum," as opposed to the comparative freedom of restorative justice, which is a sharing of different questions and a process of listening that helps wrongdoers process their actions with the understanding that these actions do not define the person.

"I SAY THE WORDS ALL THE TIME": OLD WORDS, NEW MEANINGS

While I started my individual interviews by asking student circle keepers to define "justice" and to define "restorative justice," I also provided time for them to share words they had learned or relearned through their RJ training and circle facilitation. What I loved about this question was that I had no idea what to expect; I thought SCKs might offer terms related to racial justice that emerged from their training with TRANSFORM. However, SCKs talked about words that were already part of their vocabulary but took on more critical meaning as they engaged in RJ work. One word that was consistently discussed was "confidentiality":

> I think the biggest word that comes to mind, or the biggest two words, I should say, is "community" and "confidentiality." Confidentiality is one of the biggest things in restorative justice. You know there are a lot of times where we've had more than one group [in circles], and sometimes confidentiality wasn't necessarily a problem, but it would have been obvious that if we didn't stress [confidentiality], it probably would have extended outside of the room. You never really notice until you say something about [confidentiality] how much people can continue to carry whatever happens in here [to the outside]. I think that's one thing. But "community" also, because I never really thought about the "whole" affecting everyone else thing . . . Like one conflict between [people], I never really thought that it would affect the whole school community and everyone else around, but being in the circle you realize

> how many other people it did affect. Like parents who were taking time out of work . . . students, principals, everyone, and it kind of hurts us all when students can't get along. (Kerry, May 8, 2014)

Confidentiality to Kerry was "obvious" until underscored in the context of an RJ circle. Merely reminding stakeholders that "confidentiality" is a guideline for the work helped people make a shift from being ambivalent about sharing with others what happened in the circle to a fiduciary agreement that what happened in the circle remained in the circle. As a facilitator, I have reminded stakeholders in circles that we can share the wisdom and new ideas we generate in the circle with others outside of it without attaching personal stories and names.

In many ways, "confidentiality" and "community" were related. Kerry admitted that the notion of "community" became more apparent to her when she saw how one conflict required the time of so many others, including Kerry in her role as a facilitator and parents who had to leave work. Kerry was the first student circle keeper to mention parents and families and their roles in the process. Other SCKs chose two words as well, with "confidentiality" often being the first:

> I already knew what "confidentiality" meant, but as I [facilitated] more circles, [confidentiality] became more apparent to me. And, like, not even in the circle only, but, like, outside of the circle it made me realize, like, when a friend tells you something and they're like, "Don't say anything" . . . like, how important it really is and how much it should be stressed, I guess. So that was, like, one of the big ones. And then "responsibility" too. I've learned responsibility since I was in elementary school, but there are different points of view [about]

> responsibility. There's taking responsibility for your actions, but there's also responsibility of, like, helping solve a conflict. So in the circle the circle keepers have a responsibility to be honest and help have stakeholders realize what the problem is and make agreements. Participants are responsible for what they did, for their actions. Teachers or adults are responsible for keeping it civil and, like, organized and all that. So it's like I've realized all the different roles of responsibility, I guess. ("Charlize," June 5, 2014)

Charlize made a connection between her use of confidentiality in circles and her way of enacting it in her friend groups. Through her work as a student circle keeper, Charlize found new meaning when a friend said, "Don't say anything." Given how social media makes it nearly impossible to ensure privacy for anyone, a new way of engaging what it means to honor confidentiality could be useful for adults and children alike. In fact, Kennedy staff lamented over the increased number of conflicts in the school that started with a Facebook or Instagram post or a tweet. Breakups were broadcast and bad hair days were now for all to see, and negative social media exposure prompted many students to come to school with the intent of confronting the person who posted or tweeted. Although I did not receive formal data about the effects of social media during my time at Kennedy, administrators told me that social media incidents often created conflicts among girls at the school.

Viola was another student circle keeper who discussed how she took the word "confidentiality" for granted, as well as the ambiguity of the word "respect":

> Well, one of the words that I relearned would be "confidentiality," and I feel that it's very important because, like, before, you know, everyone says, "Oh this is confidential and

> da-da-da, don't tell anyone." But with restorative justice I feel like I've learned the actual meaning of "what's said in here stays here." And I feel like that's something that people today, I guess, really need to relearn, because it's a lot of stuff that [gets out], and most people want it confidential. I would say another [word] would be "respect." Because it's a lot of times we hear "You should respect this," "You should respect that," "You should respect him," "You should respect her." As an [SCK], I saw that a lot of [students were] showing a lot more respect with two peers, [as opposed to] having a teacher telling you "You shouldn't do this" or "Why are you doing that?" Whereas, with [SCKs], students are more open to talking about why they're doing this and why they're doing that in a more respectful way. So they don't feel as if they're, like, being targeted or something. (June 5, 2014)

The word "respect" gets thrown around a lot in schools. Everyone knows they want respect, but not everyone is clear about what respect means to others. I have found that adults in school buildings expect to receive a type of respect that seems to accompany compliance. What I have not found as much are schools where adults believe that respect—showing and giving—should be mutual with students and their families. Poppa Joe, the lead poetry teacher highlighted in my ethnography *Writing in Rhythm*, often made it a point to tell students he respected them and that he respected their work.[17] I argued that when students received "respect" in their writing class, it aided them in respecting themselves or showing care for themselves and taking pride in the work they produced. At Kennedy "Jay," too, coupled "respect" and "confidentiality": "'Respect' and 'confidentiality' have kind of come back. I [knew] them and [put] them in the back of my head for, like, future references. They've come back now. Like, 'confidentiality' really sticks out, because our [school community coordinator] will tell us what happened in this room was confidential. And we do, like, stick to that. My mom asks me about [circles] and I'm like, 'I can't tell you'" (June 5, 2014). Jay stored the words "respect" and "confidentiality" but did not give them much thought until he began his work as a student circle keeper. Underscoring the importance of confidentiality as practiced in the circle process is the fact that Jay could not even tell his mother about the content of the circles he facilitated.

Jussie chose two completely different words, "punishment" and "harm," and offered his definition of the role of these two words in his community and his newfound meaning:

> I think . . . words like "punishment" and "harm" and those things. I knew about [them] . . . I know a lot of people in my community are raised the same kind of way: you get a punishment for doing something wrong. But we never really looked into it. You knew yourself punishment didn't really work, but, like, you didn't really think about it. Then, when we talk about it in training for restorative justice, then you realize why it doesn't work and how often it doesn't work. It's not [that it just doesn't] work for you. [Punishment] doesn't work for anybody. And that kind of like opened your eyes to it, and it makes me not want to just punish or just snap back for things, because the other person never really learns anything from it. It makes me [have] a lot more conversations and stuff like that. You think of the words that you're saying, and you understand how much it could hurt somebody, or you understand they might not even be in the place to be hearing what you're saying right now. And you're just wasting your time and your breath and making yourself upset. So it is; it's helped me a lot with that kind of stuff. (May 8, 2014)

Jussie's response points to the need for more research examining the role of restorative justice in communities, including the perspectives of parents and guardians of students who get involved in restorative justice at school. Jussie's reflections of the role of "punishment" in his personal life and community exemplify the critical thinking and associated critical vocabulary developed by RJ circle process practitioners. A critical vocabulary that employs restorative justice discourses can begin to help stakeholders reimagine what respectful communication sounds like. Jussie's response was one example of how SCKs made paradigmatic shifts that allowed them to engage differently with peers and adults, even beyond the RJ circle. The circle, then, becomes a rehearsal space for longer-term practices of communicating effectively, for questioning and challenging disciplinary norms, and for being in relationship with others in ways that are respectful and humane.

"IT'S TAUGHT ME TO NOT BE SO JUDGMENTAL": LIFE BEYOND THE CIRCLE

As a scholar and teacher educator who has spent a great deal of time in schools over the last decade, I am always amused when someone (typically a fellow educator) warns me that class is about to end. It's as if they expect me to seek shelter from the stampede of students rushing to their next class or getting caught up in whatever social situation awaits them in the hallway. I welcome these moments of transition, which are humbling (no one cares about grown-ups in a secondary school hallway) and allow me to witness the rhythm of the students and see some of their personalities outside the classroom. Kennedy's hallways seemed wide, even though they were lined with lockers, until students started pouring out of the classrooms and filling them up. There is a large open area in the middle of the school that many students pass through between classes. School resource officers and administrators were often located in this area, greeting students and lost visitors, like myself. I have been in schools where the presence of these professionals in the hallways felt antagonistic, but I did not feel that way at Kennedy. I noticed how frequently student circle keepers mentioned "the hallway" or the "halls" when discussing social networks and peer groups. I had almost forgotten how central the halls and passing through them are to school culture and the social worlds of students. As I made notes of SCKs discussing their hallway interactions, I learned that they viewed the school's hallways as sites where the work of RJ circles was enacted and translated into everyday interactions with peers. Because I interviewed Viola, Taraji, and Jay on the same day, and the three of them talked about the hallway, I started to pay more attention to this important site.

Viola was respected by teachers and had many friends throughout the school. In a sense, school worked for her. It would have been easy for Viola to criticize peers who were struggling learners or displayed what were deemed "antisocial" behaviors. However, in her role as a student circle keeper, Viola learned about the complexities and contexts of her peers' lives, and she learned that being judgmental only kept her from knowing people:

> Being an [SCK] has taught me so many things. I've learned a lot about so many people that I would see in the hallway and would not know, "Oh, you're dealing with that" or "You guys are having this problem." It's taught me to just not be so judgmental and to basically keep my opinions to myself. As [with] my relationships with other teachers and staff, being a circle keeper has had me meet different people here that I probably wasn't aware of ,and with that it has helped me to, like, build networks whenever I need . . . someone to talk [to] about

> [something]. And it's, like, helped me to realize that . . . we have a lot of staff here that are very supportive. (June 5, 2014)

Being able to see and engage with someone in the hallway in ways that she had not thought possible was one of the many benefits of being a student circle keeper. In addition to connecting with peers in the hallway, Viola acknowledged that many members of the staff were also committed to restorative justice culture—and that these adults were worth knowing.

Taraji had a similar perspective about building a broader network and spoke of being viewed as a role model in her experiences interacting with peers beyond the circle: "And it's nice to, like, see them in the hall and say, 'Oh, hey. What's up?' Like they want to talk to you. I just find it really cool, so it's good to know that you can be, like, a role model to other people in the school and in your community, because you're that person that they can look up to or you're that person who helped them when they needed help" (June 5, 2014).

Other SCKs echoed the value of being practiced at crossing perceived identity group "boundaries." For Charlize, this boundary crossing also applied to her relationships with adults at school:

> I made new friends through [the training process]. And then by doing circles I met a whole bunch of new people. Like when I went to the elementary school, I met teachers there and I met people [who] also went to [another high school], and so I met people there. [So] it's just like everywhere you go you know that you're going to make a difference there . . . I guess it's just like I feel like I'm actually making a difference in the community. I've always liked to serve and liked to help others in the ways I can, so I guess it's—for me it's more of like actually being able to put my words into actions in some way . . . So through restorative justice I've not only gained friendships

> with kids, but I've also gained friendships with adults too—like I can trust them. (June 5, 2014)

Charlize underscored the freedom of movement SCKs experienced through participating in trainings and being invited to programming at other school sites. This movement allowed them to develop relationships with students and adults (chaperones, activity sponsors, etc.) and build a network beyond Kennedy High School.

As I thought about students who could have experienced isolation or even removal rather than being given the opportunity to remain in the space and learn how to use language to make things right, I thought about the power of connecting these students with peers and adults who supported them in this community-building process. Students who may have experienced harm also see SCK peers in the hallway, in class, and around town, and know that these peers know their backstory and might take a few minutes to check in. Through this powerful work with and between students, hallways became another practice ground where students could engage in participatory democracy and become more active citizens of their school community.

Jay suggested that his work as a student circle keeper positioned him to act as an "upstander" (rather than a passive bystander) and amplified his voice if he witnessed wrongdoing:

> I'll leave the circles and, like, walk through the hallways, and I'll see something we just talked about—like one of the negative things. And I'll think in my head, like, "Why are they doing this?" Well, I'll actually go [over], interact, and, like, tell them to stop, and that's something I would never do [before], but it happens. And like in sports, you know, people talk stuff to each other, so it's like I'm one of those people now who would be like, "Come on, let's just focus and not talk stuff. We

> can talk stuff after." But usually I'd join in. I'd laugh about that, but it's helped. It's helped me a lot. And [RJ] shows a lot through almost everything I do. (June 5, 2014)

Jay expressed that his work as a student circle keeper "shows a lot" now in almost all of his interactions with peers. In the past he might have engaged in teasing and trash talk in sports, but he now tries to redirect his peers, because he knows trash talk can lead to unnecessary conflict. Jay also noted that he has evolved in terms of seeing himself as a leader who can influence his peers when he sees something negative happening: "[For] example, if I'm in the circle with another African American . . . I can be a good leader; [not] so they can follow, but [so] they can see what they can do through me. You know what I'm trying to say? Like, if I can do it, they can do it too" (June 5, 2014). Jay was very careful with his words; he did not want to suggest his African American peers needed to "follow" him, but that his peers sometimes get a new sense of what is possible through Jay's own actions and attitudes.

FINDING FREEDOM

The student circle keepers who participated in this study clearly found new freedoms in (1) their use of circles to demand "equality" and a space to be heard in the school community, (2) assisting peers with productive problem-solving, (3) using their knowledge of restorative justice to bring restorative impulses and responses to their work in Youth Court, and (4) (re)defining themselves or learning about their peers in order to (5) remove real and imagined social barriers to develop unexpected relationships. "Freedom" was a value that Kennedy as an institution tried to inculcate through strategies as varied as morning announcements inviting students to reflect on and exercise their personal beliefs, efforts to introduce students to the restorative justice paradigm, and a commitment to cultivating student leadership. These were all ongoing signals that reflected the leadership's belief that young people had the potential to teach the adults in the building. The role of student circle keeper gave students at Kennedy opportunities to approach relationships with a restorative impulse—moving toward people to get to know them beyond convenient (or inconvenient) identity makers or labels. While SCKs offered a compelling vision for equality that required both students and teachers to redefine their roles in learning communities, I knew that the process was not always smooth, and I wondered if most of the adults in the building shared this vision of equality and democratic engagement. Members of the staff who completed restorative justice circle facilitation and openly endorsed a restorative justice paradigm agreed to spend time with me so that I could learn more about their experiences and their views, which I describe in chapter 4.

CHAPTER 4

"THERE WAS NO JUSTICE"

Pedagogical Portraits of Educators

I opened this book with the story of Shakara, a student at Spring Valley High School in South Carolina, being violently removed from her classroom by a school resource officer. Kennedy High School also employed a police officer charged with supporting the school community; Officer Gold's title was "education resource officer." One distinguishing feature of Kennedy's journey to reimagine school discipline was that Officer Gold introduced the school to the restorative justice paradigm, which he himself learned about through community policing. When Officer Gold started to work at Kennedy, he knew many of the African American students and their families from his work in their communities. When he witnessed struggles between these young people and teachers or staff persons, he focused on how to create systems of support to address the problems as opposed to administering punishment and furthering police action. He encouraged Kennedy staff to get to know the students, see them as young people, and not typecast them. Officer Gold told the administration that they needed training in something called "restorative justice," and—under the leadership of a social worker, Officer Gold, and Mrs. Luz, the school community coordinator—that was what they did. Mrs. Luz recounted: "I learned about restorative justice from our [education resource officer]. I had only been here for a week and he said, 'Mrs. Luz, we need to do restorative justice and Youth Courts.' I had no idea what he was talking about, so I said, 'Okay!' [Officer Gold] has known some of our kids since they were tiny, because he worked in their neighborhood. He thought they needed something else" (October 2, 2012).

This chapter uncovers how educators at Kennedy worked to create and sustain a restorative justice culture in their school community. Throughout the chapter, I use pedagogical portraits to demonstrate how RJ training and implementation influence how school staff talk about work with their students, the students' families, and the students' communities, as well as what educators view as the major thrust of their restorative justice work.[1] First I provide some background about Kennedy High School and a description of some of the work these educators and I did together prior to their interviews. I then turn to the voices and experiences of seven educators (five of whom you will hear from in this chapter and two of whom are discussed in chapter 5) who were deeply involved in the practice of restorative justice at Kennedy.[2] Interviews were conducted during staff lunch breaks—sacred time—therefore I offered to provide lunch.

A quote from the forty-fourth president of the United States, Barack Hussein Obama, greets everyone who walks into Kennedy: "I believe that for all our imperfections, we are full of decency and goodness, and that the forces that divide us are not as strong as those that unite us." This quote characterized Kennedy for me; a sense of decency and goodness permeated the school's culture. I observed that a majority of students and staff in the building really wanted to be there and do right by each other; each served in the capacity of "worthy witness" of a restorative justice process gaining momentum and poised to grow and improve.[3] Kennedy came highly recommended by colleagues and other folks in the community when they learned of my research interest in restorative justice in education contexts. I always loved that the front office at Kennedy was *not* a front office; it was a "Greeting Gateway."[4] This was a paradigm and discourse shift I initially struggled with, and whenever I referred to the "front office," everyone kindly corrected me with "You mean the Greeting Gateway." When I walked into the Greeting Gateway, I was always greeted by a generous woman, "Ms. Dolly," who, like Mrs. Luz, was an alumna. Student assistants were eager to escort me wherever I wanted to go and quite disappointed once I figured it out on my own.

Mrs. Luz was the first person I met at Kennedy. She is a White woman with deep ties and commitments to the school; not only was she an alumna, but several of her relatives were as well, and a handful of them worked at the school in various capacities. In fact, when I first met her, I did a double take and had to look back at the woman whose desk is directly outside Mrs. Luz's office. Before I could say anything, Mrs. Luz said, "That's my sister! We get that all the time!" As I sat in Mrs. Luz's office, I could not take my eyes off her bulletin board, which was covered with prom photos, graduation portraits, and candid photos of young people enjoying student life. I could not help but notice that most of the photos captured celebratory moments for students who appeared to be African American. As a former teacher, I knew these wallet-sized photos were highly coveted and typically reserved for people the students really liked. "What exactly is the role of the school community coordinator?" I asked Mrs. Luz, who had twenty-five years of teaching experience in middle schools. She looked me and said, "I mostly work with African American children." I was relieved to find someone who was willing to be straightforward and decode titles and language in the schools. Much like other schools in that district, Kennedy had been disproportionately suspending African American students and had been asked to respond to this discipline gap and to the low graduation rate for this demographic.

Kennedy was considered a "diverse" school. Enrollment data from the 2016–2017 academic year shows that Kennedy's 1,558 students self-identified as follows: American Indian (1 percent), Asian (5 percent), multiracial (10 percent), Hispanic (22 percent), African American (22 percent), and White (40 percent). These categories have many unsurprising limitations. I met many "Asian" students who were Hmong, and "African American" students who were children of West African immigrants, and I never heard any students refer to themselves as "Hispanic," but I did hear "Mexican American" or "Latino/a." Like other schools, Kennedy employed race/ethnicity categories for data collection using the language and categories made available to them, including "English language learners" (27 percent) and "low-income" (56 percent). Kennedy staff and administrators considered their school and community to be a special corner of a city known for its competitive university and popular sports teams. In some ways they acknowledged an "otherworldly" ethos of their school community in that they chose to confront race and inequities overtly, as opposed to embracing the popular narrative that this environment did not experience the same issues around race and racism as larger schools and larger cities often do. My timing could not have been better; upon my arrival, Kennedy had committed to training their administrative team in restorative justice, and I was invited to participate.

WHO WERE YOU AT YOUR WORST AS A STUDENT?

Sitting in circle with administrators from Kennedy was an illuminating experience for me. I seldom thought about administrators as former teachers or as being vulnerable. Early in my teaching career, I often thought my work with children ran counter to the objectives of my administrators. We used different discourses, and I thought they were out of touch with the children and their lives. However, as

I sought to support system changes, I had to unlearn the classroom teacher versus administrator dynamic and find ways to get everyone not only to come to the table but also to engage in ongoing dialogue about how to best serve students, their families, and their communities. When Kennedy offered me an opportunity to co-facilitate a restorative justice training program for their administrators, I did not hesitate to commit. One morning in a community center just far enough away from the school so that everyone could feel "away" but not "too away" in case of an emergency on campus, administrators and support service staff gathered to engage in restorative justice community training for facilitators and to learn more about the literature on restorative justice. In one of the first rounds of circle keeper training, we responded to two questions: "Who were you at your best as a student?" and "Who were you at your worst as a student?"[5] The first question felt lighthearted and all of us seemed eager to share, but the second one prompted long pauses, deep sighs, and more tears than anyone expected. One administrator even said, "You know, the more I talk about this, the more I realize I did a lot of the things our students do. Maybe worse. I think that's why I'm so hard on them."

Training adults in the Kennedy school building was more difficult than training students. First, there were logistical concerns. It was difficult to find substitutes for administrators, and at least one administrator needed to be in the building at all times. Training teachers was complicated as well. Teachers worried that having a substitute teacher for consecutive days could undermine progress with individual students or classroom communities. While the district schedule included weekly in-service days for teachers, restorative justice training had yet to be prioritized. I believe that teachers should be paid to complete RJ training, and, if possible, preservice teachers should be trained during their teacher preparation programs.[6]

Classroom teachers at Kennedy seemed supportive of restorative justice; teachers certainly relied on student circle keepers to support their efforts to build community in their classrooms and to repair harm. It was also not unusual for teachers to call on an SCK to facilitate a circle with the entire class when tensions were palpable. SCKs were viewed as helpful in getting their peers to actually listen to and hear teachers. Very few classroom teachers, however, were themselves trained in restorative justice. When I asked teachers who talked about the subject whether they personally had received training, they typically answered, "No, but I know what it is" or "I know about it." Social service providers at Kennedy—school psychologists, social workers, and staff in roles like Mrs. Luz—found restorative justice to be a sensible extension of their work and a tool they could use weekly, if not daily. Similarly, athletic coaches found RJ circle processes to work well with their team-building activities. Administrators at Kennedy were supportive of restorative justice as well but were cautious and continued to use other methods—Youth Court, suspensions, expulsions, and law enforcement—as insurance or as backup in case restorative justice didn't work or was not deemed a suitable response to harm. In other words, Kennedy had not completely made a paradigm shift; like most school systems, no one could imagine a school community that didn't have an option to suspend or expel students.

"I'M A NON-SHARER": THE COACH

"Coach Denz" towered over most everyone when walking down the hallway. He was a joyful man who did not let anyone walk past him without speaking. He seemed to bring out the best in people, as evidenced by the way students and staff alike smiled when they saw him. The coach had been introduced to restorative justice during his first year at Kennedy, 2010: "I started to hear about restorative justice and restorative justice practices. And it was one of those things that you hear other people talking about . . . trying to help kids and adults kind of build relationships, restore relationships." In 2012 Coach Denz had an opportunity to participate in a training and started to think about how he could use the RJ paradigm when thinking about his work with student athletes. He believed the process could further his efforts, as well as the efforts of the other coaches, to "challenge our kids critically" and "make our kids think." As a former student athlete, Coach Denz believed that athletics give students opportunities to be engaged and that, through engagement, young people become part of something that matters to them:

> You gotta find something that you can be a part of. Kids who are a part of something have more success in school. They have ownership. There's a pride factor that "I'm a part of this athletic program at Kennedy." "I'm a part of the band at Kennedy." And, if nothing else, it gives them something else to come to school for [or] there was no justice, nothing to be a part of . . . Athletics gave them another opportunity . . . to engage, and it allows adults and kids to have conversations about what's going on. What can we do to help them engage? What do they like? (October 16, 2014)

Coach Denz considered schools to be unjust spaces for many students because of their inability to understand the role of citizenship and belonging in school communities—especially for students who experienced other forms of marginalization based on race/ethnicity, socioeconomic status, immigration status, or gender. The coach equated justice in schools with generating extracurricular options that captured the imagination and passion of students. He was adamant that adults in the school were responsible for making sure every child was part of something. Restorative justice, according to Coach Denz, was a tool to address the wrongs of a school culture that allows certain students to remain on the sidelines, as well as a tool to cultivate students' sense of membership and citizenship in their school community.

Much of Coach Denz's affinity for restorative justice grew from his first training, which devoted time to talking about Indigenous—especially First Nations peoples of Canada—communities' contributions to these ways of being in relationship with others. "The way [RJ] was rooted in the Native American community, and some practices started in *our* community, spoke to me . . . The historical piece spoke to me." The cultural-historical context for restorative justice anchored the coach's work and helped him situate the concept within rich cultural traditions from which everyone could benefit. In his Midwestern context, Coach Denz learned the history of First Nations peoples of Canada sharing their tools with Americans to form the basis of restorative justice in Midwestern states.[7]

However, the coach was skeptical about implementing restorative justice techniques at first, and he had every right to be. Educators are inundated with new programs, practices, and guidelines for their work, and Coach Denz forthrightly told me, "Honestly, when I first went to the meeting, it was like, 'Here we go with another initiative. [Laughter] Right? Here we go with another initiative. Let's see how long this one is gonna last" (October 16, 2017). The coach was also concerned about the sharing aspect of RJ circle processes and responding to questions in rounds. "Ironically, I'm not historically a person who shares a lot," he said, referring to his first circle. However, a group of committed colleagues made him want to commit as well: "This group of people that I work with . . . are committed, and they are a special group of individuals. And I felt comfortable enough that I could share with them because we're working toward something . . . We're trying to figure out what works best for kids and how do we help them. And so I really feel that from an athletic standpoint that there are kids that we're reaching . . . That's part of our job" (October 16, 2017).

Coach Denz distinguished between sharing for sharing's sake and sharing "because we're working toward something." I am constantly asked by preservice teachers, as well as teachers who are in the early years of their teaching careers, about how to find community in their schools or how to galvanize a movement if only a small group of people are initially interested in adopting restorative justice. Coach Denz's account of being encouraged by a small cadre of committed teachers speaks to the transformative potential of educators with shared values who begin the work together and continue to grow. While his RJ work was carried out with the support of a collaborative community, he also had a personal calling to restorative justice based on his belief that too many male student athletes receive unhealthy gendered messages about ignoring feelings and emotions:

> I find myself opening up more and more with kids, and sharing things, because they think they're going through something that's new, that no one else could possibly go through the things [they] are going through. As an African American male, especially, with sharing those things . . . [they] are typically guarded, like I was. I was taught growing up that men don't cry, men keep their feelings to themselves. And those things aren't good for you. They are not good from a health standpoint, and they're not good for relationships . . . And I think it helps those kids to know that there is a different way that I can work through things. I can use my words and we can communicate. We can figure out and get through things. (October 16, 2017)

Referencing his lived experiences as a Black man, Coach Denz named the consequences of hypermasculinities that potentially silence emotions. The coach wanted the student athletes he worked with to be effective communicators both on and off the field. He used words such as "restoring," "communicating," "trust," and "building" or "building relationships." While he was obligated to abide by the Athletic Code of Conduct for students, he believed the restorative justice paradigm could be worked into the way he and his colleagues framed expectations for student athletes and in times when there was conflict. For example, when a student athlete violated the code, Denz and the other coaches were required to adhere its policies. However, in addition to disciplinary action they could not avoid, he and the other coaches would initiate an RJ circle to show this student that he or she would always be part of the team, were valued, and were wanted back. As I observed and learned from Coach Denz, I thought about his ability to create this culture within the confines of specific top-down policies he had to adhere to. I also thought a lot about how he had opened himself to the possibility and the practice of this work largely because he was in community with likeminded fellow educators.

"THE KIDS ARE ALWAYS TEACHING ME": THE SCHOOL PSYCHOLOGIST

"Ms. April's" office was cloistered in an area that seemed like sacred ground to students. Students entered and exited the social service office suite with ease. A staff person was always there to ask what students needed and then direct them to the right person or solution. Like many Kennedy staff members, Ms. April had rainbow decals with the word "Welcome" both outside her door and inside her office. Her voice was soft, yet she spoke with conviction. Almost as soon as we sat down, she asked if she could read something to me. I, of course, said yes, and Ms. April shared a definition of restorative justice that one of her colleagues had circulated after attending a training: "A circle is a versatile restorative practice that can be used *proactively*, to develop relationships and build community, or *reactively*, to respond to wrongdoing, conflicts and opportunities. Circles give people an opportunity to speak and listen to one another in an atmosphere of safety, decorum and equality."[8]

Ms. April held on to this definition and used it as a compass for her work as a school psychologist. Acknowledging the work of Officer Gold, Ms. April continued: "I'm sure you've heard, Officer Gold brought restorative practices and justice to Kennedy for us. And many of us were involved with a first training with Kay Pranis" (October 16, 2014). The Pranis training marked a turning point for Ms. April. Pranis is recognized as a leading restorative justice theorist and practitioner in the context of how the United States has adopted the paradigm building on the work of First Nations people. Prior to her training with Pranis, Ms. April was not certain as to how or when she would integrate restorative justice into her work with students. During training, she learned that the questions through which she framed her own practice as a school psychologist were closely aligned with the work of restorative justice: "How do we support students? How do we keep students safe? How do we also keep good boundaries?" (October 16, 2014). Like Coach Denz, Ms. April was inspired by her colleagues and what they learned about one another in trainings. There seemed to be a consensus that in RJ circles one shares not merely to share but also to engage in building futures, taking risks, and using one another as resources to establish a participatory climate.

As Ms. April positioned herself to embrace the restorative justice paradigm, she was catapulted into the work when a group of students needed a way to process their feelings about a peer who had purposefully caused bodily injury to herself. This group, who were friends with the injured student, were "pretty strong students academically," recalled Ms. April. She facilitated circles around that issue at least seven times over the course of an academic year. "As you know, membership was very fluid and flexible, as circles should be.

And people came as needed, but there was probably a core group of eight students who came to most of them" (October 16, 2017). Ms. April valued the freedom of circles; she knew if she facilitated them consistently, there would always be students who would take advantage of the opportunity. Because of this new but deeply held value, she developed a tactical goal to prevent administrators from relegating restorative justice only to students from historically marginalized communities or students who were experiencing academic struggles; instead she would instill in her colleagues the belief that circles and restorative justice work should engage the entire school community.

Prior to my study, Kennedy employed the RJ circle process for truancy, and many educators interviewed for this study, including Ms. April, reported that the process went against the values of restorative justice because the practice made the truant student feel more isolated. Ms. April used this as an example of why framing restorative justice as work for one specific "offense" or type of student is problematic: "The kids are always teaching me things. One of the challenges we've had . . . was doing circles for students who are struggling with truancy . . . And not to say that we can't continue to do those . . . but there's so many layers to it . . . And when we had that narrow focus with truancy, we were not successful [using RJ] with conflict, direct support, or support around a specific issue" (October 16, 2014).

Ms. April herself used RJ circle processes in many contexts, including circles of support for the growing number of emancipated minors in the school, "perfectionist/highly anxious" students who were "never on the teachers' radars as having a problem," students who experienced depression, and ninth graders who were starting their high school careers with "a fairly strong negative self-perception and self-image" (October 16, 2017). In the same week as our interview, she had even facilitated a circle of support for fellow staff members. In other words, she wanted restorative justice to be the preferred method of communication and relationship-building throughout the school.

> My job is about relationships and about building trust, and my ultimate goal is to help kids to not only feel better about themselves but [to also develop] self-efficacy . . . [Eventually], that internal voice [in their heads] stops being mine and becomes their own, and that's the beauty. One of the great things about high school is that they're here for four years. So many students I get to see from freshman to senior year, and the transformations are incredible. [RJ circles] are very equalizing, collaborative ways to talk to one another. (October 16, 2014)

In her capacity as a school psychologist, Ms. April used restorative justice to work side by side with students in "equalizing" and "collaborative" ways. She observed students who built skills that let them transition from leaning on her more experienced, external voice to naming their own needs and figuring out how to get their needs met. While she and other staff who worked in the social services unit found restorative justice to be an important extension of their work, teachers frequently reminded them that their work looked different from that of classroom teachers because they had the luxury of spending one-on-one time with students. Ms. April spent as much time as she could in classrooms to remind herself of classroom teachers' work. Her thoughtfulness and attentiveness to everyone's feelings really stayed with me after our interview. She seemed poised to make things work more smoothly at Kennedy. Ms. April considered it her job to support not only students and their families but her colleagues as well. Restorative justice discourses were instrumental in her efforts to support the teachers and students at Kennedy; she wanted every stakeholder to make the shift to thinking about how "harm" impacted everyone: "I never make kids apologize, because

I think a fake apology or non-meaning apology is worse than not getting one. Repairing harm, repairing the wrong—we do this by actions and not just words. I always prep kids [for circles] ahead of time . . . working with students, language-wise, and even to process" (October 16, 2014).

Like student circle keepers, Ms. April used restorative justice to enact a rereading of harm and questioned the impact of a "fake" or "non-meaning" apology. While apologies are often symbolic and even preschoolers are often required to apologize, this practice can be pushed further. What does apologizing mean? Do we want the act, or an action? Replacing an apology with "What can I do to make it right?" signals accountability. Educators like Coach Denz and Ms. April employed restorative justice discourses to talk about their roles and responsibilities with students. Ms. April also saw restorative justice as an opportunity to provide this new critical vocabulary and to bolster that vocabulary with actions that signaled to students the importance of community, relationships, and mutual respect.

"WE NEED TO FIND DIFFERENT TOOLS": THE DEAN OF STUDENTS

When I sat down with "Dean Chris" the day before Halloween in 2014, she began to recall her first training in restorative justice, two years earlier. She struggled to remember what she had learned about First Nations peoples in Canada, but wanted to acknowledge this history early in our conversation. I met the dean at the RJ training for administrators, where she greeted me with a firm handshake and broad smile. She walked with a confidence I always attribute to athletes. Whenever I saw her, I noticed that she acknowledged students and staff with the same warmth as Coach Denz exuded. As dean of students, Chris had grown increasingly concerned about how social media platforms such as Facebook and Instagram make building relationships more complicated (a concern also highlighted in chapter 3). "You know, a lot of communication is remote," she explained, "and it's a different environment when you're face-to-face and there's some mutual guidelines and respect" (October 30, 2014). This truth plagued other staff members as well. The cheerleading coach told me that every student on the school's cheerleading squad was required to link personal Facebook pages to the school's page. Administrators then spent a fair amount of their time monitoring students' posts and interactions in the late afternoon and evening—posts that often led to conflict the following day.

Dean Chris began her career as a school counselor before she moved into administration. Although she had received RJ training as a counselor and embraced what she understood to be a mind-set based on how people can be in relationship with each other, she did not feel comfortable facilitating RJ circle processes when she was in that role. "I don't think a lot of counselors lead [circles] right now," she said. "But I definitely think it should and can be used more in that setting. We need more confident facilitators in that area" (October 30, 2014). When she moved into her role as an administrator charged with dealing with "discipline," Dean Chris found herself wanting and needing to access her RJ facilitator training and knowledge. A little over two months into the academic year, she had facilitated seven circles with students, staff, and families of students. When I asked what issues these circles addressed, she listed "physical altercation," "reduced suspension," "theft," "truancy," and "social-media harm" as the major topics. She seldom had time to engage in RJ community-building circles and found herself using circles to respond to and repair harm. As with most secondary schools, things move so fast at Kennedy that administrators often felt behind. For Dean Chris, the mere fact that she was using restorative justice at all was a major accomplishment that she understood as being part of her larger commitment to the young people and staff.

Chris made the case that it was counterproductive to keep punishing and dealing with every incident in school and each student involved in a silo: "We have this big urban high school. It is hard to Band-aid kid, kid, kid, kid, kid. But if you can make [RJ] a cultural aspect to your school—[RJ] is what we do and this is how we go about it—it trickles and you can see change . . . I see this as a very systematic process that can be rolled into our classroom, the way we do things, the way we resolve things" (October 30, 2014). Acknowledging that the "Band-aid" strategy was not comprehensive enough and not sustainable, the dean was pushing her colleagues to think about the long-term transformative benefits of an established restorative justice culture. She and Ms. April shared the vision that everyone at Kennedy would eventually agree that restorative justice was the paradigm that all interactions should operate from or that it was the school's core value system.

Like student circle keepers, Dean Chris found that power dynamics shifted in circles:

> I really do feel like they see me as an equal at that point. Not as an equal—I mean they know who I am and they know what I do—but I mean we don't talk about it that way. I don't, at least. I don't know what other people do. I don't go there and when I get the talking piece or [my turn] to talk about it, I don't say, "Next time you do this . . ." That never even comes up. It's a conversation: "You're a senior." "You're mature." "You need to be a leader at Kennedy." It's more of a coaching aspect, I would say . . . more of mentoring than disciplining. (October 30, 2014)

As the dean was talking, I noticed the turn she made from describing her work in circles from conversing to coaching. Providing students with images of themselves as leaders with the ability to demonstrate self-discipline was part of her approach to circles. However, she acknowledged that Kennedy still used suspensions, especially for incidents characterized as "violent." Even so, she believed that the most serious incidents should also include an effort to use restorative justice to communicate about the future, as opposed to allowing the incident to define the student: "And [RJ] doesn't mean at the end we don't say, 'We just can't have a school where we have violence.' It's not, 'If you do this violent thing again . . .' I don't bring that part in. I leave that for the day they were suspended. We talk about what will happen if this happens again. I don't really think it has a place in the circle, to be honest" (October 30, 2014).

Dean Chris distinguished the act of suspension from the RJ circle process. Kennedy was not going to abolish suspensions, so she found another space where she could use an alternative strategy to engage students who were involved in wrongdoing; she did not believe you had to forsake one for the other:

> I just think [RJ] is a different environment and [circles are a] different way of reaching a student. [RJ circles] are also a way for them to see me in a different light. [Students] see I am trying to be on *their side* and trying to advocate in different ways for *both* students. And to kind of [demonstrate] as a human being "this is what we don't do" and "this is how we want to carry ourselves and be people." And it's not coming from a stance, once again, of just punitive. It's about making you a better person, and I'm gonna be in your corner if you're doing the right thing . . . [RJ circles] are a support system, I would say, more than "I'm there to make sure it's done right," or "I'm checking the boxes," or whatever. It's more about "I have opened myself up to you to know that you can come [to me]." The kids I work with in the circle now know that "I can trust her." (October 30, 2014)

In the restorative justice paradigm, Dean Chris could communicate that she was an advocate for *all* stakeholders instead of taking one side and completely isolating or labeling students who caused harm. She alluded to how the perfunctory aspect of her work—making sure things are "done right" and "checking the boxes"—might seem to be the extent of her work. However, this focus on punishment sets up the dynamic of a two-tiered system of worthiness and deservingness among students. Chris believed that all students deserved to know that they could trust her, and her deeper goal was to provide a scaffold for communication that gave students the tools and vocabulary to imagine a positive future.

Dean Chris said that most of her restorative justice work was with freshmen who were unfamiliar with Kennedy's culture:

> It's freshmen who we don't know yet, exactly. So that's a time that they get to see me, and I'm not out to get you, we're not out to get you. We just need safe behaviors in our school. And we need you to be safe. And what comes out of it, too, is other things are divulged in a circle that gives us [opportunities] to provide other sources or resources and interventions. Stuff I didn't know about, [students] are willing to bring out [in RJ circles]. I had a girl the other day say, "My past has not been good," and she divulged some things, and we really talked about the confidentiality of the circle. This led that other student to say, "Well, mine hasn't been either, and this is what I've gone through." That triggered me when I left the circle to say, "I'm gonna get you hooked up with [name of a counselor]. I think this will be a good person for you to talk to." So that was kind of what came out of it as well, another intervention strategy. Another thing that was brought to light and a little bit of a root cause as to why maybe [those students] went down that path, for us to kind of deal with them and help them get some resources. (October 30, 2014)

Walking me through this recent RJ circle she had facilitated, Dean Chris demonstrated how the circle process gave two students who were in conflict an opportunity to define themselves beyond the incident in question and to learn they had more in common than they knew. It also prompted her to get both students the resources they needed to better understand themselves and become their best selves.

Dean Chris ended our interview with one of the tensions and challenges Kennedy was experiencing: teachers needed more training, and just because they knew about restorative justice did not mean they knew or understood how to use it as a tool. I found that teachers at Kennedy did not share the pedagogical stances described in chapter 2 like other members of the staff; they thus still approached their work with students in "punishment" mode. Chris was baffled that students were being sent to her office for talking in class, but this pattern affirmed her belief that the adults in the building had to be on the "front line" and active leaders in the process of shifting this paradigm:

> I mean it's hard for [students] to adjust to knowing [administrators] are part of the process. You need to be part of the process. You are the front line. And that's been difficult. We've had some teachers that have [sent] students [who were] talking in class to us. And I'm thinking this is where we need to start—in the classroom. This is not what we want—kids to lose learning. We need to find different tools. I think one thing we need to really do is help our teachers [and] give them more professional training in actual intervention strategies that they can use and feel comfortable with . . . I feel like there's an uncomfortable level for some teachers knowing how to process things [using RJ circles], and they need some training and guidance on that. (October 30, 2014)

In many ways students and administrators were working with tools that, quite frankly, many of the teachers did not yet possess. This gap in restorative justice knowledge and training generated obstacles in establishing an RJ culture, and RJ was often the scapegoat for tensions that were more aligned with organizational structure.

FROM "GRAND PLANS" TO "OLD HABITS": THE ENGLISH TEACHER

When I asked Mrs. Luz to suggest nominations for classroom teachers who were working toward a restorative justice mind-set and practice, the one teacher whose name consistently came up was "Ms. Reese." This petite woman was often indistinguishable from students until one spotted her Kennedy lanyard and heard the jingling of keys. Before becoming an English teacher, Ms. Reese had worked part-time as a positive behavior coach, and in this capacity she learned about Youth Court.

I sat with Ms. Reese a few different times, as it was challenging to fit her interview into the breaks she had during the school day. She began our first formal conversation by telling me about the time she had seized a restorative justice training opportunity during the previous school year: "Most of our training was in a circle . . . so we got to experience it and we got to reflect on our lives as high school students. [We] actually got to meet some of our students, some of our circle keepers, who guided us through a couple of [rounds]. We got to see how students lead" (October 30, 2014).

Admittedly, the process felt a bit "awkward" for Ms. Reese and "didn't come as naturally right away." Despite this awkwardness, she believed that the more she practiced, the more it would become "natural": "There was a time when all of the staff were sitting in a circle and we were crying. We were sharing these experiences from our youth that impacted us. Why we do what we do today. We used the concept of throwing a rope to students, and we shared experiences of when we threw ropes and the kids held on and we pulled them onto the right track and times [when] it didn't work. So that was fantastic. I learned the most from that part of the training" (October 30, 2014).

In this training, circles were used to convey purpose, history, and a sense of how the educators in the circle had gotten into the profession of working with children. What brought them to the work? By historicizing herself as a learner, Ms. Reese realized one of the areas that often yielded a disconnect between herself and her students:

> I think I became a teacher because I really thought about myself as a high school student. That's when I really started to figure out who I was, and I wanted to be part of that for other kids. But I was also a goody two-shoes. I was the kind of kid who did all the work, got all A's. So it's difficult, I realize as a teacher, it's very difficult for me to connect with kids that had a very different experience and different motivation levels than I did. And that is where I am trying . . . to come up with strategies and see things from youth's perspectives that are very different from my own experiences. (October 30, 2014)

Elsewhere, Power Writers program cofounder Joseph Ubiles and I recount our work with preservice teachers.[9] In our workshops and in methods classes, we invited student teachers to create footprint maps highlighting the sites where they acquired language(s). When working with English teachers, we found that most of them had memories of reading in the laps of parents, spending time in libraries, and were students who just "got it." Like Ms. Reese, the English teachers we worked with struggled to understand students who did not enjoy school. They found comfort in traditional narratives of being read to and being in print-rich environments, and they believed that students who did not share these experiences were disadvantaged. Ms. Reese was ready for a new lens. When she was having a difficult time communicating with a student, she enlisted the help of a student circle keeper who facilitated a circle that included another teacher:

> It's very uncomfortable . . . I felt like the kid was a little bit uncomfortable. I was a little bit uncomfortable. We made some progress towards the end, and his response was that he really liked it and he felt supported. 'Cause in the end we mostly focused on ways that we could help him be more successful and help him stay focused. So I think once he realized that we all cared this much to sit down and talk about this with him, he started to put forth more effort in class. (October 30, 2014)

Ms. Reese's willingness to name her discomfort was important. Restorative justice circles are not neutral, and the structure and function can make people feel vulnerable. In this case, Ms. Reese noted that when the student realized that everyone was working on his behalf, he became more fully engaged. This notion of sharing for a purpose, talking for a purpose, and thinking together toward a purpose is what keeps the circle going. Ms. Reese continued to reflect on this student's growth:

> And in fact the truth is that we made almost 100 percent—I mean he changed a lot, and he actually started doing his work in class, started doing homework, coming to ask for help. Anytime he'd start goofing around in class, I would just kind of be like "Uh, oh. Okay, okay," so we had this connection between us. And so a couple of times when [colleagues] asked me to share, I actually got emotional, because I couldn't believe the change that I saw in this kid compared to the beginning of the

> year. So even though I was like "I don't know if that circle did anything, it was awkward, I'm not sure if I'll do it again," obviously it impacted him, and he was able to find meaning in it and make a change. (October 30, 2014)

In the case of Ms. Reese and this student, change was still the responsibility of the student, not necessarily the adults who worked with him. I wondered what kind of pressure this student felt in trying to demonstrate change. I recalled my work with Girl Time, the previously mentioned playwriting and performance space for formerly incarcerated girls. At one point while I was interviewing student artist participants, I had a clarifying moment because I continued to get similar responses from girls about how they planned to move forward with their lives. I asked about specific changes and noticed that this fed into a discourse of personal responsibility that did not acknowledge the myriad factors that contribute to children's decisions (or their indecision). I altered my question to "What changes need to happen around you so you can thrive and live the life you desire?"[10] This is a very different question, and it is a question that should enter RJ conversations in educational settings.

Ms. Reese felt defeated, to some extent, because this story did not end the way she hoped:

> Unfortunately, the story doesn't have the best happy ending, because at the end of the year he sort of reverted back to the beginning of the year [in terms of his behavior], and then he wasn't interested in doing a circle. So it's kind of funny because he did not pass first quarter, he got A's and Bs second and third quarters, and then he dropped off at the end. And my only sort of interpretation with that is perhaps he realized that the end of the year was coming; he was starting to put up those defense

> mechanisms, because he knew that . . . I was trying to analyze it probably too much. But I think we made a difference, and the fact that he has half a credit of English was better than not doing the intervention. (October 30, 2014)

By this point, Ms. Reese embraced a restorative justice mind-set despite her disappointment about "losing" this student. She realized after this experience that she did not want to save circles for moments that were difficult but wanted to integrate them throughout her practice:

> I haven't incorporated it as much as I wish. I find myself having all of these grand plans at the beginning of the year and kind of reverting back to my old habits. But one of the things that we talk about is that I sit in the circle. We're all equals. At this point we are all learning from each other. Every single person's voice is important. A lot of times a classroom will become imbalanced; three or four kids will talk the whole time and the other kids will kind of close up. And so this is an opportunity for everyone's voice to be equal and get to know each other, because we need to feel comfortable making mistakes around these people, because when we make mistakes that's how you learn. And so you feel more comfortable making mistakes around people that you know and that you know will support you. (October 30, 2014)

Ms. Reese and her students generated "work agreements" in circles, and she started introducing curriculum in circles as well so that students were comfortable and *she* was comfortable. She was very aware at the time that the district would soon implement a new plan to deal with school discipline, and the plan encouraged "restorative practices" such as circles, conversations, and the like. Ms. Reese explained how she was preparing for this change by working on her mind-set:

> I knew this plan was coming. I prepared myself. I knew that I had to create an environment that prevented [conflict] from coming up. Last year I had students that if I'd had them this year I would have no idea what to do. All they did was come in the room and curse everybody out, say, "I'm not doing this" or "This is so stupid" and "I hate you." They would leave the room, come back five minutes later, and this would happen every single day without any consequences. I was very, very afraid that this was going to happen again this year. I knew I had to start from scratch [in] building relationships with kids, being demanding or the warm demander. And making sure that kids understood how they were to behave in my room but also feeling like they were a member of a community where they wanted to behave because of the people in the room and for the purpose of their own learning—not because I wanted to control them. (October 30, 2014)

Ms. Reese's attitude and response to the schools new conduct code, a strategy for school staff and students that insisted teachers find ways to keep students in class rather than sending them out for minor issues (which pleased Dean Chris, who had been wary of teachers sending students out for talking in class). The new code underscored the work of paradigm shifting. Though Ms. Reese had not received any new training since the previous school year, she was determined to cultivate a classroom environment where students desired to be in the room. In other words, she considered herself responsible for proactively helping students experience the classroom community as a positive experience. She took up the pedagogical stance that she wanted students to understand that both stakeholders wanted the same things:

> "I want what you want. I want you to be surrounded by friends. I want you to be in control of your own destiny. I want you to be good at things." These are all the things they want, right? In order to do all those things, though, they need to be nice to people in the classroom. The need to make good decisions, because, ultimately, they are in control of their own destiny—and so we had lots of really good conversations that I never had with my students before. (October 30, 2014)

Ms. Reese employed a restorative justice discourse whereby she appealed to students' desire to be free, to have control of their present and future selves. She admitted that she had never had these conversations with students before the district made it clear that they would no longer accept students missing out on learning time for issues that could potentially be handled in the context of a classroom. Reese saw circles as a "venue" to "create those relationships" and said that her "classroom management philosophy" had become "just building those relationships":

> Before, [students] started to push the line, when they were still sitting there ready to figure out what they were going to do in this classroom. I just made sure that it was really apparent and that they knew I was not here to control them, and that I am here to help them become more successful. I think that started it, and I've been more consistent with expectations. I actually made my expectations even higher. We talk about language in the room . . . I don't say I'm going to kick them out of the room if they use bad words, because that would be ridiculous.

> But they know that the reason they need to use better words in the room is so that we create a positive environment and we don't offend each other and bring the morale down. I definitely started off the year a lot stronger than I had in the past. (October 30, 2014)

I found it compelling that when Ms. Reese started to make a paradigm shift that focused on language, purpose, and community, she *raised* her expectations of students. She also demonstrates an educator's role in establishing accountability. Much of the criticism of restorative justice in schools focuses on whether students are being held accountable. I think we should also consider whether educators are holding themselves accountable in this work. Ms. Reese realized that in adopting a critical vocabulary around expectations with her students, she had to raise her expectations and more effectively communicate those expectations.

"I'M NOT GOING TO QUIT ON YOU": THE ASSISTANT PRINCIPAL

Assistant Principal "A. P. Jake" always wore his signature uniform: a white button-down shirt, a green tie to show school spirit, a dark-hued sweater vest, a pair of slacks, and, like most of the staff, a Kennedy lanyard around his neck. It had been twenty-four years since Jake had been a classroom teacher, but he drew from his teaching experiences to talk about restorative justice and building a restorative culture at Kennedy High School:

> The way that I perceive restorative justice and restorative practices is a patchwork or a wide variety of things, some of which live here at Kennedy. We've done some peer mediation programming, and I think restorative practices in the early days felt to me that it was just as much about the adults as it was

> about the students receiving mediation. It was a way for us to get off being on the soapbox, always in charge and running things, to us really being with our students. It benefits students who find themselves in relationship struggles. In another sense, it is really important for the school culture and climate, because we create leadership opportunities for school. We have fifteen hundred students here, and some of them are basketball players and some of them are in the foreign language club. You have to find your niche. For our kids who are [SCKs] . . . those are student leadership opportunities that, if you do not seize upon and do not cultivate, I think that not only do those programs not develop and flourish but your leadership can also go from positive student leadership to negative student leadership. (November 6, 2014)

A. P. Jake helped me understand why Kennedy was committed to the student circle keeper model as opposed to beginning their restorative justice work with the staff. He saw restorative justice as an opportunity to cultivate student leadership, and, much like Coach Denz, he believed that every student in the school building had to find some activity, club, sport, or way of being that gave that student a sense of school community membership. Jake believed that students are the true leaders in schools and that he and his colleagues had to learn how to capture the positive leadership qualities that all students possess. He was relentless about engaging the staff with this asset-based perspective:

> I continually tell teachers, even pre-[RJ] era, that I can probably discipline kids into compliance *maybe*—but I'm never going to be punishing them into engagement . . . So when we have students who are able to function in *this* classroom and then two periods later are falling to pieces in another classroom, then

> let's look at our triangle. If what we're doing isn't really working for eighty-five percent of our students on a consistent basis, then we need to get some Tier 1 issues we need to address. (November 6, 2014)

The "triangle" Jake mentioned is a figure used by schools to demonstrate that the foundation of restorative justice—the base of the triangle—should be community-building "Tier 1" restorative justice work. School districts such as California's Oakland Unified School District assert that Tier 1 community-building RJ work should be used with 100 percent of the student population. The midsection of the triangle, or "Tier 2," is for restorative processes or processes that occur after harm has taken place. In the context of the Oakland Unified School District, only 15 percent of the student population may need these kinds of processes. Finally, "Tier 3," or "supported re-entry," includes restorative justice circle processes that welcome and reintegrate students who had been removed from schools. The district suggests that Tier 3 should be used rarely (for approximately 5 percent of the restorative justice work). In sum, more foundational RJ "community-building" work done from the outset should replace the need to follow up with more serious actions later.

Jake knew the difference between "compliance" and "engagement." The last thing he wanted to do as an administrator was spend a lot of time disciplining students into compliance. Punishment does not lead to engagement, and compliance may be short-term if a student still does not have a sense of belonging in a school community. Jake led with this, and even when I gave him hypothetical scenarios and role-played teachers who did not feel they had time for restorative justice in the classroom, he pushed back:

> So our new policy says that [teachers] are going to have to deal with issues, skillful teachers who are intentional about building

> classroom environments that value learning, empower individuals, that are authentic and meaningful . . . Student voices are in the process . . . and are in places they tend to thrive. And when we flip the page and go to systems and structures that are punitive, I ask [teachers], "Does your system give you what you were hoping it did?" "Do you get a sense that your system has allowed your classroom to thrive and you've leveraged grades into positive discipline?" [Because] a kid gets into a spot where it's hopeless and [feels], "There's no way I can pass your class, because I've had my cell phone out" . . . so now we're in a spot where you don't have any leverage over me and my behavior, and "I'm not going to pass your class anyway," and you don't want me in a spot in October, and I can't pass your class because—new policy be damned [laughter]—because I'm going to make you lose. So we want to avoid power struggles because in that we're going to lose. (November 6, 2014)

A. P. Jake mentioned to me that his first job was in a homeless shelter. He described a scene where it was him, sixty homeless men, and one homeless woman in the shelter, and how he had made it a point to develop relationships right away, anticipating that there would be both good and difficult days. This work informed his education philosophy: "I want to be sure we got each others' backs. To me, that was my classroom setting as a teacher, and as a principal I'm going to hold the bar high. I'm going to know who you are. I'm going to expect a lot out of you. I'm going to set shorter horizons for you if you are struggling, and I'm going to reinforce those expectations. I'm not going to quit on you. I think many of our staff are there" (November 6, 2014).

Like Ms. Reese, Jake emphasized the need to "hold the bar high" and make sure students hear "I'm going to expect a lot out of you." Acknowledging that some students might need short-term goals, he believed students need to be thinking about next steps beyond the situation right in front of them. This, he was clear, is the responsibility of the adults in the Kennedy building.

SHIFTING THE PARADIGM AT KENNEDY

When I consider these educators' pedagogical portraits of restorative justice at work, I think about the pedagogical stances that are present, as well as absent, in how they approach their work. To be sure, History Matters was articulated by each of these educators when they considered how Kennedy started building a restorative justice culture. Even those who did not know Officer Gold well knew that he was the conduit for restorative justice at Kennedy. Some educators also historicized their own lives to situate their RJ work. A. P. Jake talked about his very first job and having to find ways to cultivate relationships with individuals who had little evidence that they could or should trust him, while Ms. Reese relayed her experiences as a "goody two-shoes" student and how that life experience had a negative impact on how she viewed students who struggled with academic learning. Coach Denz talked about the support he received from coaches as a youth and how this mentoring and sense of belonging at school established a sense of "justice" in terms of making students like him—who did not feel they really belonged—matter.

Race Matters, the second pedagogical stance, was not addressed as openly as I imagined, given that during my first interaction with Mrs. Luz, she was comfortable telling me the school had created a full-time position to focus on African American students. What Ms. April did not say in her interview, but what I clarified with her later, is that the students she practices restorative justice with were primarily White, and when she referred to students who were "not on teachers' radars," she was talking about White students. Many people assume that restorative justice is used solely for students of color, and that is irresponsible. Coach Denz, as an African American man, lamented that race and the monolithic box that cis-gender heterosexual males tend to find themselves in can be deterrents to open communications that convey emotion and seek to collaboratively solve problems. In chapter 5 I address more aspects of in-school tensions around race, with attention to what was spoken and unspoken.

Justice Matters was implied, but not leveraged, by all the educators profiled in this chapter. Ms. April explicitly told me she preferred "practice" over "justice," because she felt that "justice" was inextricably linked to the criminal justice system. The criminal justice system has monopolized the word "justice" in a way that negates the work of seeking fairness and equity. Coach Denz had an interesting perspective on "justice," which he felt was strongly linked to membership and belonging. He considered schools to be morally and ethically obligated to make sure there every student had a club, activity, team, creative endeavor or a just a place to belong in a school community and that anything less was unjust. Dean Chris alluded to justice when discussing her role as an advocate for "both sides" in restorative justice circles and her goal of making sure every stakeholder knew she was there to support them and identify resources.

Language Matters was probably most visible in these profiles. First, educators at Kennedy used restorative justice discourse; phrases such as "repairing harm" and "building community" were used frequently. Most of these staff participants mentioned focusing on "relationships," and Ms. Reese was explicit about changing the discourse in her classroom to encourage participatory democracy by asking students about their needs and desires for a classroom community. Ms. April talked about making sure actions and words were aligned as an alternative to "fake" or "non-meaning" apologies. The administrators, Dean Chris, and A. P. Jake used additional examples of affective statements that emerged in restorative justice circles, reinforcing a discourse that helped these educators to coach, mentor, and encourage students to be their best selves. The orientation to language in restorative justice circles was future-oriented, with the goal of supporting students beyond the circle.

These are not neat and tidy findings. As I stated earlier, my desire is not to present a perfect story of restorative justice in a school community, though I do aim to grapple with the work—and shifting toward a restorative justice paradigm is a process. What Kennedy had was a core group of students and educators who believed in the work and remained committed. However, even with a committed group, there are still questions that emerge from the tensions and challenges of this work. What does it mean for students to take on responsibilities as student circle keepers? Why are most of the circles at Kennedy, except those facilitated by the athletics department, facilitated by female staff? Whose work and responsibility is restorative justice in schools? Such questions, and the tensions that fed them, are the topics to which I turn in chapter 5.

CHAPTER 5

WHEN SOME OF US ARE BRAVE

Tensions and Challenges

Viola, the student circle keeper whose words inspired the title of this book, was one of my greatest teachers during this project. Finding time to interview her was a challenge, as she had several leadership roles and was active in multiple venues across campus. When asked how her peers and adults in the building would define her, Viola offered the responses "a positive individual" and "a hardworking student." It was evident to me why she was often chosen to represent Kennedy High School in forums off campus that required student speakers or participation; she was an eighteen-year-old with presence who made eye contact, smiled easily, exhibited kindness, and spoke with conviction. From my vantage point, I could see her being held up as an example that Kennedy was having some success with African American students.

However, Viola's labor came at a cost. During one of our interviews, she was visibly upset and tearful when listing the many student groups she was involved with and events she was expected to attend. "I missed PE again, and my teacher is so nice. He said he understood and supports me, but I don't want to miss his class. I just want to enjoy being a student for the little bit of time I have left here." We ended the interview and talked about how she could respectfully decline invitations. Viola continued to express her desire to be a "regular teen" and to be more present for what remained of her senior year in high school. When Viola contacted me the summer after her freshman year in college, she and I met for coffee. She was still involved in campus life, which she described as "the norm" at her historically Black college/university. She did not, however, feel the need to belong to every student group or participate in an overwhelming number of activities and could thus prioritize being a scholar. "There's a lot of students just like me [laughter]," Viola explained, "so I don't feel as if I have to do everything."

The student circle keeper experience at Kennedy gives students like Viola an opportunity to participate in the school's effort to practice justice. She and her peers were familiar with the perspectives of their fellow students and considered themselves assets to the restorative justice movement in their school. It bears noting, though, that the SCKs I interviewed were primarily African American girls. In some cases, these girls were involved in other efforts in the school and for others, but the SCK role created a leadership opportunity they did not have otherwise. The purpose of this chapter is to confront the pattern of restorative justice as girls' and women's work or the work of people of color in schools. Drawing from empirical data of my study of RJ work at Kennedy, I address what is at stake if most of the students and staff trained in restorative justice circle processes are girls, women, or people of color, and female staff are responsible for most of the work. What are the consequences of producing/reproducing gendered justice—that is, the feminization of peacemaking and making things right? I will first examine how student circle keepers who identify as "female" experience their role as restorative justice circle keepers and how they position themselves and their labor in relationship to the school community. Student circle keepers who identified as "African American girls" experienced their roles as SCKs in three ways: (1) circle keeping as advocacy, (2) circle keeping as reflective, and (3) circle keeping as representative. I will also consider the roles of women on Kennedy's staff and, in so doing, uncover how much of this restorative justice work became their responsibility—and how often the work felt unsupported.

While I maintain that training students as circle keepers is a way for schools to leverage the powerful resources they have in their students, I also believe that any school using this model must send a clear policy and must practice signals to demonstrate that this student labor is valued. Students can often see and name contours of the school community that tend to be unseen or not experienced by the adults in the building. I posit that if students are to have such responsibility and provide such labor in school, they should also have the power not only to define the terms of restorative justice work in school policies and practices but also to shape school culture. Furthermore, all staff should be trained instead of relegating RJ work to a few adults in the building. Lastly, restorative justice work should not be allowed to become a net for everything that needs to be done for students, nor can those doing the work be overburdened with it.

REVISITING "BETWIXT AND BETWEEN" LIVES

In their groundbreaking edited volume *But Some of Us Are Brave: All the Women Are White, All the Blacks Are Men*, Gloria Hull, Patricia Bell-Scott, and Barbara Smith contend that Black women's "legacy as chattel, as sexual slaves as well as forced laborers, would adequately explain why most Black women are . . . far away from the centers of academic power."[1] One of the major thrusts in compiling a wide range of scholars and practitioners to set the stage for the field of Black women's studies was to establish the "recognition of Black women as valuable and complex human beings."[2] The provocative title these scholars chose for their book alludes to the reality that Black women in the United States have been marginalized in freedom struggles yet continue to resist oppression and excavate sites in which they can be fully human. Like their predecessors, Black girls today have been silenced, stereotyped, and criminalized in classroom and school communities, often living lives "betwixt and between" freedom and confinement, as discussed in chapter 2.[3] Stories of betwixt-and-between lives are starting to gain traction in historiographies. In a study of Black women's labor titled *Labor of Love, Labor of Sorrow: Black Women, Work, and the Family, from Slavery to the Present*, Jacqueline Jones makes the point that even when Black women were "freed" or "liberated" from "narrow gender-role conventions," they still had "little leverage": "As spiritual counselors and as healers, black women did exert informal authority over persons of both sexes and all ages in their own communities. Yet when measured against traditional standards of power—defined in terms of wealth; personal autonomy; and control over workers, votes, or inheritances—black wives and mothers had little leverage with which to manipulate the behavior of their kinfolk."[4]

Throughout this book, I revisit Shakara at Spring Valley High and how the racing and gendering of the incident she was involved in allowed onlookers to doubt her integrity, despite a video showing state-sanctioned violence against her and her body in what was supposed to be a learning community for children. One of Shakara's classmates, Niya Kenny, who spoke on her behalf and questioned Officer Fields's response to Shakara, was also arrested under the Disturbing Schools statute (see introduction). Kenny's witnessing and advocacy were punished, prompting the American Civil Liberties Union to file a complaint.[5] I found it ironic that with African American girls being the fastest-growing group of students to disproportionately experience suspension, expulsion, and other forms of isolation in schools, student circle keepers at Kennedy primarily identified as "Black/African American" and "female." Kennedy depended on Black girls' labor for their restorative justice work.[6] Playing on a recent book and film about a community of African American women who work as maids for White families, I call this "the help" factor—that is, Black girls and women are often viewed as helpers or confidantes and relegated to supporting cast roles in the workplace. When I interviewed Dean Chris (see chapter 4), she told me she had received more referrals for African American girls to participate in conflict circles than any other group in the school community. At first glance, this does not seem to be a big deal. If a Black student or students are at the heart of a conflict, a student circle keeper with a shared ethnic/racial background facilitates a circle process. This sounds reasonable, but this strategy is dependent on the assumption that all Black students can and will relate to one another.

Perhaps more dangerous is that this strategy does not hold the entire school community responsible for finding ways to be in relationship with one another. Are Black students the sole responsibility of their peers, Black staff members, or White women who are willing to do the work? Who owns this work and why? What are the implications for other learning communities? In her examination of child protection and the notion of innocence, Erica Meiners argues that restorative justice is not enough—that is, in most schools, restorative justice is delegated to one or two people in the building rather than upheld through a culture that is cultivated through shared values and practices.[7] Is it possible, asks Meiners, for the "anti-school-to-prison pipeline work that is rooted in restorative practices" to uproot zero-tolerance policies? I extend this query to ask about the cost of the labor being put into building a restorative justice culture in a school community and whether this labor will ultimately be undermined.

"THEY WOULD RATHER OPEN UP TO US": CIRCLE KEEPING AS ADVOCACY

In chapter 3 I wrote about how student circle keepers at Kennedy High School were introduced to restorative justice work using a racial justice lens in the training they received from TRANSFORM, a nonprofit organization that has an explicit mission to eradicate racism. In this training, SCKs learned about racial disparities in school discipline policies and practices both locally and nationally. Therefore, they were exposed to restorative justice discourses that called for equity in educational contexts. Mary was the first SCK to explicitly refer to some of the conversations she knew to have taken place among Kennedy staff:

> I don't know if we're supposed to know this, but I found out that [Kennedy staff] actually had a sit-down talk about how there's more Black kids getting sent to the office with referrals. Instead of writing [students] up, just send them to the office so they can talk to their principal. So the numbers were so bad. But I feel as if when you don't have restorative justice for kids that have already done something wrong or . . . [are perceived to be] disrespectful, and they don't come to us, 'cause they've already dealt with the police or something like that. [Students] should still come [to circles] . . . They look at what kids already have referrals, and if I've had a referral already they're not gonna let me come [to circles] if I get another one. (May 8, 2014)

Mary named some of the tensions that schools in the beginning phases of implementing restorative justice experience. She had some understanding that her school disproportionately punished Black kids ("the numbers were so bad"); however, she also noted that students were being sent to the police or receiving some form of retributive justice before participating in a circle process. This inconsistency signaled that Kennedy was not entirely confident in their process and that staff were selective about who was worthy, so to speak, of the circle process and the opportunity to make things right. Students received mixed messages, as some were referred to SCKs while others received more traditional punitive actions.

Nina (self-identified as "African American" and "female") said she believed it was important for African American students who were referred to "conflict circles" to see an African American face, especially as a facilitator:

> Restorative justice is not just for a certain ethnicity. Sometimes [there are] more African American [students] in circles. But that's where we come in . . . I've done circles where it's me and another African American [student] with the adult. I feel like [the African American student] would rather open up to [African American circle keepers], and they're more honest and feel like we understand them. So I feel like that's where we come in and kind of help students of color, because they can open up to us. I feel like they can open up to us a lot more. (June 5, 2014)

Nina's observations are indicative of the challenges and potential tensions of training students as student circle keepers. The leadership opportunities are undeniable; Nina appreciated the opportunity to engage in RJ work, especially when African American peers were involved. While Nina asserted that restorative justice was not for a "certain ethnicity"—a point made by school psychiatrist Ms. April in chapter 4—the reality was that she saw more African American students than White or other students in circles.

Other SCKs also suggested that African American students were being referred to RJ circles for "conflicts" more often than other groups on campus. Student circle keepers seemed to be able to make the paradigm shift (see chapter 3) quickly; it seemed to me that most of the African American SCKs had the restorative justice mind-set—even those who never found themselves "in trouble" like their peers. I also noted that African American SCKs often mentioned facilitating circles with only one student, or "single circles." I began to wonder how much the school depends on African American SCKs to do communicating that, quite frankly, the adults should also be learning to do. Where were the other stakeholders? Where were the advocates for the stakeholders who needed to build consensus? I have had this debate with colleagues who are RJ practitioners, and they maintain that the adults in the school building need to be held accountable for this work; it should not be the sole responsibility of students.

If the purposes of restorative justice are to think about how wrongdoing impacts a community, how those who have experienced harm can have their needs met, and how those who have caused harm can get the support they need, how is this achieved in a circle consisting of one student circle keeper, one student, and one adult? A single circle, rather than community-building circles, puts students in a position where they have to locate the problem within. This is *not* restorative justice; it is, however, another form of isolation tied to a discourse of personal responsibility. While personal responsibility is important, I wonder how effective it is to use restorative justice circles that have the same objectives as in- and out-of-school suspension. Student circle keepers were essentially counseling or talking with the student "in conflict," which, according to African American SCKs in this study, was compelling, but I maintain that it is not fair for the SCK or the student in question to be held accountable in this way. For Nina to facilitate a circle properly, there would be multiple stakeholders, and in the case of a conflict, each stakeholder directly linked to the conflict would also have an advocate present. I worried that African American SCKs would take up the notion that problems are personal problems and that they pathologize their peers.

Kerry also referred to single circles. From Kerry's perspective, circles that focused on one student alone allowed her to serve as an advocate:

> I have a friend at [at a different high school] who often gets suspended because of teacher–student conflicts. He really has a problem with teachers for some odd reason. And I've wanted to do [RJ circles] because we've actually talked to some of the staff at [my friend's school], and one of his really close teachers I actually spoke with about restorative justice. [We're] not only building it here in Kennedy but building it in schools around [the city] and [inaudible] anywhere else we can get it. So I definitely think that RJ could help, because the single circles we've had have been with some African American males and females [where] I feel like them seeing [me]—especially being African American myself—lets them know that . . . even though you're a guy and I'm a girl [and] guys have different pride issues and stuff like that, you don't [have to get into conflicts]. (May 8, 2014)

Recalling figure 2.2, it is important to have multiple stakeholders to share the process of making things right. A single circle suggests that the only people who are responsible are the SCKs and the student who has either experienced or caused harm. Kerry had a unique opportunity to serve as a student circle keeper at Kennedy and potentially influence educators on other campuses. Witnessing her friend, who happened to be an African American boy, get suspended frequently compelled Kerry to speak with teachers at the boy's school about restorative justice. Kerry did not name race but said that "for some odd reason" her friend struggled to get along with the adults in his school. Unlike Mary, Kerry did not link her work to a larger narrative of racial injustice or racial disparities in discipline practices at Kennedy. Rather, Kerry pointed to gender in her retelling of her friend's story in that she believed "pride issues" played more of a role for boys than girls when it came to relationships with teachers and administrators. However, Kerry implied that having an African American student circle keeper was preferable, regardless of gender. Kerry's analysis of the restorative justice process at Kennedy was that it was reactive rather than proactive. In other words, the school administration ultimately decided who would participate in the process, making it difficult for students to distinguish the process from traditional punishment. At Kennedy, restorative justice was being used interchangeably or in tandem with other practices.

"I SEE MYSELF": CIRCLE KEEPING AS REFLECTION

Mary, the student who pointed out that at least some students were aware of some of the tensions related to discipline policies and practices at Kennedy, described her trajectory in school as "messing up on a lot of things." When Mary transferred to Kennedy her sophomore year, she quickly found her strength to be "helping other people" who exhibited behaviors similar to hers. Whereas Viola, Kerry, and Nina considered themselves academically successful and college-bound, Mary viewed herself as a student who struggled both academically and socially. Restorative justice and the student circle keeper role were tools for Mary to use and further develop her natural skills. In Mary's case, the circle-keeping process had just as much of an impact on her and her behavior as it did on the stakeholders in the circle:

> I used to have really, really bad anger problems, but that was a younger freshman year kind of thing. Sophomore year I started [at Kennedy], and it kind of changed for me, because

> I saw different lights, different situations, and I haven't been angry since. I really figured out that [helping other people] is what I'm probably best at that I don't mess up on, because I seem to mess up on a lot of things [except] being a failure and helping people. I can fail at a lot of things, but that's one thing that I know I'm really good at. (May 8, 2014)

While Mary characterized her struggles in school as a "younger freshman year kind of thing," she acknowledged that the culture of restorative justice at Kennedy presented an opportunity to redefine herself, and she seized this opportunity. Taraji experienced circle keeping in a similar way: "Since I've joined restorative justice, I see myself . . . if I get into it with someone, I just don't find it as important to tell anyone else. Like it's just, I resolved it with that person and that's all that matters. Like I don't have to tell anyone, because it's just between me and that person, or me and those people, or whoever it is. It's just between us. So I've definitely taken that" (June 5, 2014).

Much like African American girls I interviewed in the Girl Time theater program for formerly incarcerated girls, many girls at Kennedy expressed how they had struggled a lot in school, blaming themselves and using the discourses of the school to frame themselves and their behaviors. Seldom were these girls able to think about their dispositions in schools in critical ways that challenged their experiences with teachers and staff. In contrast, student circle keepers have opportunities to use each circle, the restorative justice paradigm, and their restorative impulses within the circle to rehearse for life beyond the circle. These are critical skills needed for everyday interactions and are critical for *all* students, not solely students of color. Imagine how powerful restorative justice work could be if all students participated in community-building circle processes that have the potential to serve as boundary-crossing social networks where students develop empathy for themselves and for one another as they observe and experience the full humanity of others. This is important as education continues to address inequality: "Schooling cannot instill shared values throughout the U.S. population" if specific groups of young people do not have access to quality educational experiences. Racial disparities in punishment exacerbate this inequality. Therefore, it is imperative that we find ways that schools "can create social networks that cross the boundaries of families and communities [that] help knit the fabric of American society."[8]

"So a lot of it, like, I bring up my personal experiences—like I say in middle school I wasn't the best. I was, like, the naughty kid always getting in trouble, and I really bring that out when it comes to the conflicts, because they don't feel like they can relate to anybody in the circle. And showing that I'm this facilitator, that I'm this circle keeper—that I am a leader now really shows them that they can change" (Jennifer, June 5, 2014). Like Mary, Jennifer leveraged her experiences as, to borrow her words, "the naughty kid" in order to be an effective student circle keeper. As a self-identified "White" SCK, Jennifer saw conflicts more in terms of gender than race, asserting there was a lot of "girl drama" in school. Jennifer also said that co-facilitating with a fellow SCK, Jussie, helped her gain credibility with peers and that circle participants learned more about one another when they shared personal experiences in circle. As I analyzed the interview data, I saw a trend that mirrored findings in my ethnography of formerly incarcerated Black girls. Student circle keepers who positioned themselves as having a difficult time in school were unable to articulate a critique of what was behind being "angry" or being "the naughty kid." Even so, these African American and Caucasian student restorative justice practitioners spoke of binaries such as "good student/bad student."

Charlize (self-identified as "White" and "female") positioned herself as having relatable, shared experiences with African American peers. Like Jennifer, Charlize saw her own complicated relationship with school as an asset for circle keeping:

> In middle school, I was sent [to] an alternative learning center that kids who get in trouble in class go to. I was sent there more than once, and as I came into high school I've definitely had drama with my friends. Like I'm not the perfect person, and I'm not—I don't have, like, the perfect background of never having conflicts, never having troubles in classes and stuff. I have had situations with teachers even at this school that I just, like, don't get along with them, I guess. So it's just, like, I don't have the perfect background, and because of that I can actually help people out more. And, like, my GPA isn't a 4.0; it's not, like, fabulous or anything like that. And I'm definitely involved throughout the school, and I've definitely met a lot of people throughout my classes and all of that. So I guess it's just, like, because I have the experience I do, I can help more, because I can understand where people are coming from. And I can understand the situations that they're facing. (June 5, 2014)

Charlize framed herself in terms of what she was not ("I'm not the perfect person . . . I don't have the perfect background"), which, from her perspective, differentiated her from many of her White peers. In a town known for having its fair share of residents with graduate and professional degrees, being working poor or working class and White was isolating in many ways. Charlize was almost apologetic for being White without a "perfect background."

Although Charlize aligned herself with African American peers, this positioning did not demonstrate a nuanced understanding of her African American SCK colleagues. For example, Viola and Taraji excelled in school, both academically and socially, and grew up in middle-class families. Charlize saw herself as being able to "understand where people are coming from" and used her experiences to try to be relatable in circles. In chapter 3 I talked about Charlize's reflections on being a student circle keeper; in addition to developing relationships with other students, she established positive relationships with adults at Kennedy through her restorative justice work. I saw Charlize with adults more than I saw her with her peers; other than Viola, I did not see other SCKs who considered staff to be "friends." Charlize's labor in school resulted in relationships with adults that afforded her other opportunities, such as babysitting and housesitting jobs.

"I CAN GET MY EDUCATION ON MY OWN": CIRCLE KEEPING AS A TOOL TO (RE)DEFINE

Three student circle keepers self-identified as "African American" and "male." Derek, Jussie, and Jay were born in Madison, and Jussie had the most experience as a circle keeper (three years). I discuss them here to address the experiences of boys who engaged in restorative justice work. However, these boys were very different from one another. Derek was focused on a career in American Sign Language and had plans to attend a college where he could continue his studies. Jussie was outspoken and charismatic; he was focused on being a scholar and was viewed as an RJ leader, much like Viola. Jay was under the radar; he just wanted to live his best life, smile, and be everyone's friend. He was a person of few words, but he was warm and funny.

Derek did not mention race/ethnicity until the end of our time together. The entire district was suspending Black students more than any other community of students, and Derek was one of the few Black males in a visible leadership role that wasn't linked to sports. Although Derek did not talk about how this affected him personally, he did want to talk about how the punitive culture affected his friends and other Black males he knew on campus. Derek expressed that he wanted to see more African American students in circles and implied that they were being suspended more than any other group: "Well, I think we could have more African American students in the circles instead of just jumping to 'We need to suspend them,' . . . 'cause I know a couple people that need to be in the circles, but they just get suspended anyway"(May 8, 2014). I asked Derek if he could say more about why he wanted to see African American peers participate in the RJ circle process with more frequency. He said that the process "could really fix the problem" before telling me that being suspended provoked more anger in his friends, who were also Black males, when they returned to school: "I know when they come back, they're like, 'Oh, they suspended me.' And I just know that it makes them more angry" (May 8, 2014).

Jussie expressed a similar concern but used himself as an example. As Jussie told me about his story of being confronted with a suspension, I must admit I was surprised. Every adult I met complimented Jussie, and he was well liked by his peers. He participated in Youth Court and restorative justice and spoke passionately about both. His personal experiences with punishment at Kennedy alluded to the fact that prior to Youth Court and RJ referrals, suspensions and expulsions had been the only tools and options for "discipline" and harm at the school. Race/ethnicity seemed to be the primary indicator of how the school would respond to harm. Because he was so soft-spoken and even-tempered, I struggled to imagine Jussie in the situation he described: "[I got] into an altercation with a student in, like, a gym class, and he put his hands on me and I flipped out. I was so upset, and I guess I said I would kill him, and I cussed him out and everything. [The] gym teacher told me [afterward] basically that even though [the other student] physically assaulted me that I would get suspended [for] verbally assaulting him. And I was like "Why am I getting suspended?" (May 8, 2014).

I was struck by Jussie's vulnerability and transparency when he conveyed how much he did not want to be suspended:

> I was a freshman and I didn't want to get suspended, and [administrators] were like "Oh, you get suspended, it goes on your record and da-da-da." I didn't want to get suspended. I had never been suspended at all for anything, and so I was like "I don't want to get suspended for reacting to a situation." And that was before Youth Court and RJ were really in the roots of the school. 'Cause that's something that really could have used a circle [process]. I really needed a circle. (May 8, 2014)

No one thinks about how students who experience punitive practices feel, because there is an assumption that students who get suspended just don't care, or they present themselves as aloof or not remorseful. Jussie provided a different perspective that demonstrated his confusion, disbelief, and fear of having "a record." He was still upset about this experience. Here he was a senior and on his way to college the next academic year, but the strain of being doubted and punished stayed with him:

> JUSSIE: And then I, like, lost trust in the whole entire school, because [I said to] the teacher, "As an adult, you let a student put their hands on me and you didn't do anything, and you are blaming me for how I reacted to that. You don't really know me, so you don't know, like, my background, but the people who have the same background as me might have reacted a lot differently and most likely would have hurt the kid." And then [the student] was also White, so then it was a racial thing, like "Why am I getting

suspended? I feel like if I would have hit [the other student], I would have been suspended already and you guys wouldn't be talking about it." And then I got called to the principal's office, because she wanted to make sure that it wouldn't turn into a "thing." [She asked] if my uncles or anyone was coming up here to fight [the other student]. And I was, like, my uncle is forty years old! Has three kids and is married.

MAISHA: Wait. What uncles?

JUSSIE: 'Cause a lot of kids here have uncles that are around their same age.

MAISHA: So there were some . . . basically, what you're telling me is there were some assumptions made [that] because you're African American you were going to bring family members to get involved and it was going to get bigger and bigger?

JUSSIE: Exactly, yeah. And I told [the principal] if I wanted to fight him, I would have fought him. I didn't want to fight him, I don't like fighting. My uncle is a grown man who has a wife and three kids, who has a house, and a boat, and a car, and he has a whole life.

MAISHA: He's not coming up here to beat up a kid!

JUSSIE: Right! He's not coming up here to fight a little kid . . .

MAISHA: But the assumption is so interesting.

JUSSIE: And that just, like, cut me off from the whole entire school. Everything. I was just like, "I can do my school for myself. I can get my education on my own." "I just don't need to deal with that." And that, like, was how I got through basically junior year, just not talking to anybody. Because I was just like, "I don't need them. I don't need to talk to the principal." I never talk to her, 'cause I don't get in trouble, so I'm, like, I don't talk to her. After what she did, I was, like, I'm done with her. (May 8, 2014)

Jussie's story stayed with me for a while. I thought about the bright children in our schools who want to engage and be engaged but who feel misunderstood and are not given the benefit of the doubt. I found it frightening that a student like Jussie came dangerously close to not being seen or heard. Jussie's talents nearly went unnoticed, and this seemingly straightforward conflict could have isolated him. I found it disturbing and unsurprising that he believed racial dynamics may have discouraged adults from seeing past his race or hearing him. Educators constantly miss opportunities to learn from and with students, and school communities throw away young lives every day. Jussie reconnected with Kennedy through restorative justice work and circle keeping, but this incident remained with him—in spite of his efforts to define and redefine himself on his own terms.

It was not until the end of my interview with Derek that he, too, shared a story about a conflict he had with a teacher at Kennedy:

DEREK: I know there are, like, a couple teachers here that just . . . that really like to take advantage of their authority. When I was talking with the teacher yesterday [she asked], "Oh, what happened in the library?" And I would try and tell [her], and [she's] like, "Oh, that's not what [the other teacher] said." And I still ended up getting a referral, and I didn't think that was fair.

MAISHA: That's interesting to me, because even though you do this work as a circle keeper, you were in a conflict with a teacher.

DEREK: Yeah.

MAISHA: And does the teacher know you do this work?

DEREK: I'm not sure. But it's not just me that has this conflict with that same teacher. It's a lot of people. And she's—this year is her first year too, so . . . I think . . . like, a lot

> more teachers actually should be more involved in the circle-keeping thing, because all my teachers don't even know that I'm a circle keeper. So I know they probably heard of restorative justice, but they don't really know. I don't think they know what it's doing for our school and the students that are a part of it, or the student leaders that are helping the other students during the conflict around the school. So I think they just . . . I think more of the teachers should be involved and should know about the restorative justice program. (May 8, 2014)

It was disappointing for Derek to be viewed as leader in his work as a student circle keeper but to be doubted by teachers when it came to an issue that came up between him and another teacher. It was as if he occupied two systems that were not in communication with each other. Derek did not know if this teacher knew about his SCK work, nor did he know if it mattered, because this teacher and many others needed training and experience. When Derek mentioned that this teacher was in her first year, I recounted a bit of the story about Antonio that I wrote about in the introduction to this book:

> MAISHA: What do you think it is about the first year? I mean, I think this is really important, and I'm trying to figure it out. I can't tell you that I know the answers. I know that my first year of teaching I think I didn't really know what to do in certain situations, especially my first year teaching high school students. Like the first time a student basically disrespected me in front of the class, I was so embarrassed. I was just embarrassed. And I felt like the other kids were looking at me like "What is she going to do?" Right? And so you felt almost like you were in a confrontation, and it really took me a long time to understand I'm the teacher

and I don't have to engage in this way. I know your situation was really different, but I think a lot of first-year teachers, they get scared and so they get defensive. Right? And then they just start making decisions that aren't always the best decisions, because they don't know what to do.

DEREK: I think that what happens with some teachers their first year, students might start to, like, push over them and might really disrespect them or something. I don't know. That could have happened with her, and now she's just like [shrugs shoulders]. (May 8, 2014)

To see these young people completely invested in their school community was an inspiration. They loved Kennedy. They wanted the school to keep growing better, and they were holding the school accountable for thoroughly embracing what every public school should be: accessible to all, rigorous for all, and welcoming to all. Their work should absolutely inspire a significant commitment to holistic transformation and paradigm shift.

"EVEN THE MOST SKILLED VODOU MAGIC TEACHERS AMONG US": WOMEN EDUCATORS AT WORK

Educators also experienced tensions related to restorative justice. "Ms. Faith" was a social worker at Kennedy during my time there; however, she had served in various capacities at the school prior to this position. When restorative justice was being implemented at Kennedy, Ms. Faith's position was "diversity director." It sounded good, but I sought clarification of the job description. "What did I do?" she said. "You name it. Everything from academics to social emotional learning. Getting kids engaged in classes. Meeting with parents. College visits. Post-secondary options" (November 6, 2014). When I asked Ms. Faith what the diversity director was charged with, she replied, "Everything!" I also wanted her to clarify what "diversity" meant, to which Ms. Faith replied, "minority."

Everybody loved Ms. Faith. Kennedy staff punctuated any reference to her with "I love her!" "She's great!" Students lined up outside her door as if they could not get enough. As a social worker, Ms. Faith acknowledged that she continued to do much of the work she had done as the diversity director in addition to working on her caseloads to help students meet their IEP (Individualized Education Plan) goals. Ms. Faith, who had been trained in multiple restorative justice processes, believed that student circle keepers were the voices of the school and were committed to changing the climate of the school. This is what I observed as well; it was evident that SCKs were invested in Kennedy. When I shared with Ms. Faith that I had not met any White male SCKs among the cohort featured in this book, or even in the cohort the following year, she, too, was puzzled. "I don't know why," she said incredulously. She just had not given it any thought—and who could, given how busy everyone was? Ms. Faith viewed her incredible workload as the norm, but at a certain point she decided she needed a break from the work, which was overwhelming. She moved to another school but could not stop thinking and worrying about specific students she had left behind.

Ms. Faith returned to Kennedy in less than a year, jumping back into her role of supporting all students, particularly minority students, without questioning the workload that had spurred her decision to take a break. Ms. Faith and "Ms. Tracee"—both African American women—were the only two social workers at Kennedy. Ms. Tracee had replaced a White woman who had been deeply involved in restorative justice but had moved on to a position in the district office. Though Ms. Tracee was new and replacing a very popular predecessor, she became immersed in Kennedy quickly, perhaps in part because she was an alumna of the school district and committed to the work. Students approached Ms. Tracee about everything, and she was concerned that restorative justice work, and circle processes in particular, were becoming the go-to strategy for addressing needs that were beyond the scope of RJ work. Ms. Tracee, a big advocate of restorative justice, wanted to see more comprehensive services at Kennedy—and schools in general; she was invested in a model where students could access all the services they needed under one roof:

> I'm hoping the direction we are going in is comprehensive services in the school that are available to students. Health services. Kids having the opportunity to talk about safe sex and those kinds of things are hot-topic issues, but we know that those things are happening, so we need to allow students to protect themselves and be smart about things. And mental health—it is important to have a clinician in the school who is working in and with the school so we're able to communicate with each other. (October 16, 2014)

Ms. Tracee also described a host of other services that were needed. She believed that rather than herself and colleagues who did not have degrees or training in some of the issues mentioned above, the school should hire appropriate professionals to serve students. She was concerned that restorative justice circles were becoming a "catchall" for anything that wasn't going smoothly in schools and that this could undermine RJ work. Ms. Tracee was trying to determine ideas and approaches that were sustainable and would support students beyond the circle process.

After my interview with Ms. Reese (see chapter 4), she asked if she could follow up with me. She had given more thought to my question about whether she might consider sharing her own process with colleagues who were trying to do this work. Ms. Reese did not feel comfortable sharing with her colleagues and being perceived as someone who figured things out. She worried that such sharing would create tensions with colleagues who were going out on "stress leave" and "calling in sick." Ms. Reese wanted to do more work on herself, her own paradigm shifting, and what restorative justice work looked like in real time: "Based on the referrals I've written over the last six years, I look racist. So I don't write referrals anymore. That doesn't mean the behaviors have stopped, but that's what the administration sees. Seventy-five percent of our school referrals are for African American students. I don't want to contribute to that, so I've stopped documenting these behaviors. It saves me *tons* of time. Our suspension records look bad too" (November 6, 2014).

Though not documenting problematic behaviors saved her "tons" of time, Ms. Reese explained that the time and energy involved with RJ work was probably the main reason other classroom teachers remained unwilling to be leaders—or even practitioners—of the process:

> I have put so much energy into reaching out, calling home, making accommodations for students who are regularly absent, supporting Saturday school, and counseling students who are struggling at home and at school. I am so spent by the end of the day that I have nothing left to give my family. And that's all before I've started to grade or plan or figure out how I'm going to pay the bills. . . . I teach reading and writing, and I work hard to incorporate social and emotional learning into the things we read, write, and speak about. What teachers are being asked to do is vodou magic. Impossible. I recently took two sick days just to catch up on grading, planning, teacher evaluation requirements, and laundry.

Restorative justice was becoming a common scapegoat for the seemingly endless list of tasks teachers were being asked to complete;

even a teacher like Ms. Reese, who saw the benefits of making the paradigm shift, "fizzled out." Despite making progress in her classroom and developing a personal strategy for communicating with her students using an RJ paradigm, she undermined her own work and struggled to resist the deficit discourses of colleagues who had not been trained in restorative justice. Teachers were overwhelmed, and rightly so; how could anyone add one more task or a new outlook to their dockets? Referring to the expectations of the teacher workload as "vodou magic," Ms. Reese admitted that she could not keep up with both her work and her personal life.[9] While grading, planning, teacher evaluation requirements, and laundry have nothing to do with restorative justice, Ms. Reese asserted that being asked to build relationships and create an RJ culture when one could not keep up with her regular work was unacceptable, unrealistic. Educators like Ms. Faith, Ms. Tracee, and Ms. Reese, who have the disposition to do the work of restorative justice and who are engaged in paradigm shifting, need more support. They cannot simply be told that relationships with students are a priority and simultaneously handed a list of time-sucking busywork that feels counterintuitive to creating expansive and welcoming learning communities. Unlike the coach, the assistant principal, the school psychologist, and the dean, Ms. Reese did not have a large group of colleagues among her classroom teacher peers at the school to bolster her work. Ms. Reese continued:

> I believe that restorative practices intend to hold students accountable, but I have not witnessed a real transformation in behavior yet. It is definitely a step in the right direction; I do not believe that detentions, suspensions, or expulsions fix things. But expecting teachers to teach content to higher expectations, aligning brand-new assessments, measuring growth through teacher evaluations, while creating engaging lessons and giving

> timely feedback, incorporating social and emotional learning standards and brand-new technology, communicating regularly with parents (of 150 students), and then complete a restorative process every time a student ditches class, flips you off, sleeps through class, disrespects others, all while being responsive to cultural differences to close the achievement gap . . . is *insane* [her emphasis]. We are simply not capable of doing all those things, even the most skilled vodou magic teachers among us.

DISCUSSION

How can we expect educators to do this work without more support and an organizational structure that supports the work? How can we show rather than tell teachers that the restorative justice paradigm and impulse must remain a priority if we don't support the work? Ms. Reese's experiences demonstrate that restorative justice work is possible and potentially transformative, but she admitted to me that she was not going to continue to uphold other top-down expectations, because she could not possibly do it all, and she did not feel she could even share best practices with her colleagues. As alumnae of the district, Ms. Faith and Ms. Tracee believed they understood what it meant to be Black in that city and in those schools, and these women planned to continue the work—even if it continued to be too heavy a load. Though their perspectives about the future of the work varied, the fact remained that these women labored for their school community in ways that we see from women educators and people of color throughout the school system of the United States.

I am admittedly conflicted about the model of training students to be circle keepers. As an educator and ally of young people, I find that training students as SCKs in restorative justice circle processes is an opportunity to provide a new generation with prosocial mind-sets and tools to be builders, problem solvers, and collaborators. The agency I observed in the actions of student circle keepers and heard in their narratives of restorative justice work is a strong foundation for leadership and a worldview that promotes healthy, respectful relationships. One challenge that must be addressed is that students are laboring in a system that will not give them power or more respect in return. Derek and Jussie continued to be haunted by the threat of being generalized and criminalized at school. If students are to be trained, then they should be part of the process of defining and determining the terms of relationships on campus. When student agency is not a determining factor in the school's structure, policies, and practices, or if adults in the building are not working to transform their mind-sets and practices, then reliance on youth labor is not justifiable in that school setting.

If restorative justice circles are to serve as a tool for creating and sustaining boundary-crossing social networks for students and staff, then everyone in the school community must be held accountable as a stakeholder. In the next and final chapter, I outline what I refer to as Transformative Justice Teacher Education, which reimagines the nature and work of teacher preparation in addressing restorative and transformative justice agendas.

CHAPTER 6

"HOW DO WE TEACH SO THAT PEOPLE STOP KILLING?"

The Case for Transformative Justice Teacher Education

Chronicling her brief and arduous tenure as a classroom teacher at "Black Hole School," Mary Rose O'Reilley asserted, "A lot that went on there was wrong by anyone's standard, but worse than the badness was the moral neutrality."[1] Acknowledging her shortcomings as a teacher, O'Reilley admittedly "fled" to graduate school at the University of Wisconsin–Milwaukee, where one of her professors, Dr. Ihab Hassan, posed the question "Is it possible to teach English so that people stop killing each other?" in the context of a colloquium for teaching assistants at the height of the Vietnam War. O'Reilley and her classmates were realizing that the grades they assigned students—open admissions students in particular—would literally determine whether these students would serve in the Vietnam War:

> My generation of teachers began to worry about grading because grading was a life-or-death proposition. We had to make some connections pretty quickly between our classrooms and the war outside. We began to change; our methods by which

> we ourselves had learned did not work for open admissions students, and we did not want our students, as a consequence of our inept pedagogy, to be killed. We began to see grading is at the least metaphorically a violent act, because in 1967, it was *literally* a violent act.[2]

Throughout O'Reilley's career she thought about Professor Hassan's question, and through her quest to create "the peaceable classroom," she has shared this quest with the next generation of educators and scholars. This question simultaneously haunts me and motivates my work. While I ask a slightly different question—"How do we teach so that people stop killing?"—I agree that educators should be concerned with the "war outside" our classrooms, including the daily trauma so many children and their families endure as a result of socioeconomic, health, political, and sociocultural inequalities.[3] However, I would also argue that educators must address the war *inside* our classrooms, where students are routinely denied access to the kind of learning that can change a person's socioeconomic forecast, self-advocacy skills, social networks, and ability to be free. The outright violence that Shakara experienced and her classmates witnessed—and all the many similar incidents that have not been recorded—creates a clear caste and class system in classrooms that makes it clear who matters and who does not. I do not feign neutrality here. I have been a witness to Black suffering and anti-Blackness and -Brown-ness in schools, and I experience a fundamental desire and yearning to disrupt the practices rooted in this denial of all children's humanity. I think about this daily, as a Black mother of Black children who I am raising to be free—free from the limitations others will try to project onto them as well as physically free.

Deeper still, some of our children face symbolic and physical violence in their classrooms. Scholars have argued that education research and policy have been unwilling to name schools as a site of suffering, especially for Black children.[4] Anti-Latinx, anti-queer; anti-immigrant, anti-Muslim, and anti-non-dominant identity in general are all deeply linked to the larger domain of anti-Blackness. So, yes, we need to "change our methods," much like O'Reilley and her colleagues attempted to do, and not allow "inept pedagogy" to be a reason we lose children. Transformative Justice Teacher Education seeks to offer a new methodology that holds our educators accountable for identifying institutional racism and racist policies that they participate in, whether implicitly or explicitly, and teaches them to resist unjust methods that render historically marginalized children unworthy of a rigorous academic experience with a sense of purpose and belonging.

Restorative justice is not a map. To borrow from Howard Zehr: "The principles of restorative justice can be seen as a compass offering direction. At a minimum, restorative justice is an invitation for dialogue and exploration."[5] Maps, of course, are useful; however, the sociopolitical terrain is changing daily, so a compass is needed to serve as a guide amid upheaval and change. This chapter provides such a compass; herein I offer a framework for Transformative Justice Teacher Education as well as a brief overview of the literature that informs this framework. I also share aspects of my own pedagogical portrait as a restorative justice practitioner, focusing on my restorative justice discourse work with both pre- and in-service teachers.

WHAT IS TRANSFORMATIVE JUSTICE TEACHER EDUCATION?

Transformative Justice Teacher Education (TJTE) is a model that views teaching as a justice-seeking endeavor and learning as both a civil and human right for all students. TJTE in the US context asks what it means to teach in the age of mass or hyper incarceration and the increasing criminalization of children in our schools, especially, but not limited to, Black, Latinx, Indigenous, differently abled, queer, trans, Muslim, immigrant, and "undocumented" children. I ask teachers to engage in the deep work they must do to unlearn racist ideas that manifest in punishing their Black and Latinx students more than their White and Asian peers. I do not stop here. I also support educators in taking the steps to understand why they must maintain high expectations for the life trajectories of *all* students and resist acting as gatekeepers with students who do not fit easily into comfortable or familiar schemata. TJTE is sincerely concerned about the children in our schools and equally concerned about their families. Here, I draw from Black community school models that have provided support, outreach, and even coursework that empowers parents to learn alongside their children.[6] This approach is well captured in a short film depicting a "restorative welcome and reentry" circle for a student at Bunche Academy in the Oakland Unified School District. At one point in the film, a circle participant addresses both the student who is being welcomed back into the school community and his mother:

> And I need for you to fall back a little bit from that man role and taking the lead, and just be a *young* man and enjoy this journey to being a man. And one thing I know so much is that you love that woman right there so much. That's your heart right there, and you would drop on a dime for your mother . . . And I know you carry a heavy load sometimes because you worry about her. You worry about your family. I know that. I'm worried for you worrying about your family, and sometimes I think you worrying about your family is the reason why you've made some of the decisions in your life that you've made. But those decisions in life need to change, because you got a network of people, and let some of us worry about that load—but you gotta tell us . . . and I need for Mom to tell us too, because we not against you, we for you . . . and we here for you.[7]

Stakeholders in this circle included advocates for the student, his family, each one of his content area teachers, and administrators from the school and district levels. While this particular circle is focused on reentry as opposed to building community, I cite it here to underscore how stakeholders in RJ circles work together to generate a community response that takes into consideration the whole child, which includes his family. Many would challenge whether schools and districts can afford to convene such a process for one student—especially a student involved in wrongdoing. TJTE, on the other hand, begins with the premise that all children and their families are worthy of this level of engagement, empathy, and compassion. We must do this work in teacher education. We need to radically reform our programs, uphold professionalism, and underscore the urgency of this community-affirming work across ages and disciplines. The humanities cannot do all the work; math and science teachers must be in solidarity. As scholar Erika Bullock points out, Shakara was in a remedial math classroom at Spring Valley High School, which means the situation there was also an issue of math equity and access.[8]

FROM "PROBLEMS" TO OPPORTUNITIES

In my attempts to reach pre- and in-service teachers as a restorative justice paradigm shift communicator, I revisited my elementary school teacher identity, drawing from the compelling nature of children's literature. To open a restorative justice discourse circle for teachers who had already been trained in RJ Tier 1 processes and wanted to deepen their practice, I read Kobi Yamada's *What Do You Do with a Problem?* to the group.[9] The protagonist asks a series of questions about his problem: "Why is it here?" "What does it mean?" "What does it want?" "What if it swallows me up?" "What if it sneaks up and gets me?" "What if it takes away all my things?" After attempting a range of avoidance responses, the protagonist concludes that avoiding the problem has made the problem "bigger and scarier than it actually was." When the protagonist chooses to face his problem, he learns that the problem actually "held an opportunity . . . to learn and to grow. To be brave. To do something." After reading this story, I ask teachers to respond to the prompt "What do you do with a problem?" Using a talking piece, every teacher has opportunities to listen and to be heard. Some teachers discuss strategies and struggles solving problems; others recount how their approach to problems has evolved since they first began their teaching careers. After this round, I invite stakeholders to process what has been shared and to add anything else they may want to share. After everyone has spoken (and the talking piece makes its way back to me), I invite stakeholders to imagine that our "problems," especially when it comes to discipline in our classrooms, are actually opportunities. I ask them to hold on to this idea for our work together.

I work with two key texts for this process and in my classes on diversity in the classroom for preservice teachers. An atypical adoption for a teacher education course, Dawoud Bey's *Class Pictures* is a collection of portraits of high school students from across the United States.[10] I find this book of photographs to be an important tool that helps educators begin the hard work of resisting stereotyping their students and assuming they know and understand individuals based on how they look, what they wear, their race/ethnicity, and other visible characteristics. I had the honor of seeing these portraits firsthand when they were exhibited at Emory University in Atlanta, Georgia. My department chair in the Division of Educational Studies wanted to hold our faculty retreat in a new space that might spark creativity and new ideas. This new space turned out to be the visual arts gallery on campus, and Bey's larger-than-life portraits were featured. When I saw the images, many thoughts went through my mind about who these young people might be. Then I saw a small note next to each portrait containing an autobiographical statement in the student's words. I quickly unlearned my own perceptions and relearned who the students were through their own words. For my teacher education courses, as well as my restorative justice discourse learning experiences for educators, I ask that everyone create a "Class Pictures" project of their own. They can use mixed media (not everyone always has photos of themselves) to generate an image of themselves when they were the age of the students they are teaching or hope to teach. Each project includes an autobiographical statement, written in poetry or prose. We hang these and have our own gallery stroll. In more intimate groups, we share the projects in a circle; I recommend this only for groups with twenty or fewer participants. For large classes (twenty-one to one hundred participants), I offer time for students to share their projects with the entire class, but sharing is not mandatory. If possible, preservice teachers in my class create projects alongside students in the classrooms where they are student teaching and make plans to exchange projects to learn more about each other. More students than I expect always volunteer to share.

The second text I consistently work with is *Start Where You Are, but Don't Stay There: Understanding Diversity, Opportunity Gaps, and Teaching in Today's Classroom.*[11] During teacher education courses and RJ discourse trainings, I ask each educator to draft a "Start Where You Are" project, in which they discuss where they are as educators and where they want to be and then create an action plan (reading lists, trainings, immersion experiences, etc.) outlining how they will get there. Numerous teacher education students later tell me they had planned to frame their practice using the teaching philosophy statement they submitted for admission into the program; however, after critically engaging with the aforementioned texts, reading Ta-Nehisi Coates, and learning more about mass incarceration, racial bias in school punishment, and restorative justice, they have determined that the teaching philosophy they started with was ill-suited to the challenges and opportunities they will face as educators.

Early in a course or training, typically on the second day, I focus on four "rounds" of questions designed to build an arc that connects teachers to themselves as young people. The first two questions are "Who were you at your best as a student?" and "Who were you at your worst as a student?" The next set of questions include "How were you and your students similar?" and "How were you different from your students?" Following these exchanges, teachers—whether preservice or in-service—often tell me they appreciated doing this work with their peers. While it depends on the school community, I have done this work with only classroom teachers or with a mix of teachers, administrators, and staff. I value interdisciplinary work and I often create opportunities for educators and scholars to work across content areas, but I find that these professionals also want and need time with people in their own field to reimagine their work with students. In some cases, teachers desire a space to process ideas, hopes, and concerns beyond the ears of administrators, and vice versa. There is also great value in periodically bringing together content specialists to discuss how restorative justice might be applied in a specific domain of learning, from the unique perspectives of each domain, as there is much to be gained from a collaborative process of thinking through best practices within one's educational niche. In the next sections, I offer some thinking about TJTE across disciplinary contexts. By no means is this exhaustive, as there is a community of scholars who are deepening and strengthening this work.[12] I aim to provide an overview and resources to begin this journey.

TJTE CORE CONTENT APPROACHES

Math

An editorial published in the *Journal of Urban Mathematics Education* in 2010 invited educators and administrators to engage a movement seeking to keep central to math education the question "Where's the math?" There scholars argue that math is not "acultural," but a tool for "understanding the world" and examining "social forces" that influence the lives of historically marginalized learners:

> Students on whom equity scholarship often focuses—African American, Latino/a, Native American, and poor students—serve as canaries in a mineshaft for the long history of content-focused scholarship in mathematics education . . .
>
> Minimal progress for these students would seem to demand that we pursue *all* promising areas of inquiry informing us about how to help them experience mathematics in ways that allow them to change the conditions of their lives.[13]

Practitioners and scholars demonstrate such possibilities with, for example, circle processes used to ensure equitable math discourse in classrooms. TJTE asks math teachers to consider who is talking, how often they are talking, and what they are being asked to talk about. Scholars have found that even in schools that promote social justice, in which teachers are passionate about disrupting inequities in their school community, math teachers still call on White and Asian students for more complicated questions and ask Black students to answer basic questions. Such patterns and norms generate "niches" for students based on race/ethnicity.[14]

Questions for math teachers to consider might thus include:

- Who am I calling on and for what kinds of questions? At what frequency?
- How can I physically set up my classroom so that all students have a chance to participate in classroom discussions and problem solving?
- How do I create a culture in which all students view themselves as "math people"? What histories might I need to access, and how do I embed those into my teaching?

Equity-oriented scholars have argued against "math hazing"—that is, a gatekeeping mechanism that determines who gets to be a mathematician and who does not.[15] These scholars propose a "Restore—Transform—Imagine" mathematics education that centers the ability to "restore" relationships between students and mathematics, "transform" the math classroom to recognize students and the knowledge systems they bring as assets, and "imagine" a mathematics education that is focused on equity and racial justice not only in schools but in detention centers, jails, and prisons as well.

Science and Agricultural Science

Because TJTE is equally concerned with teaching and learning, science and agricultural science education that focuses on teaching and learning modules for both science/agricultural science teachers and students is particularly salient. In a demonstration lesson titled "Chemistry Is Around Us: The Story of Flint," Alexis Patterson and Salina Gray invite students to "power up," or share everything they know about the water crisis in Flint, Michigan. Patterson and Gray ask students to take a series of tweets from politicians, residents, and community activists and create a timeline of events with them.[16] Ultimately, students are asked to view the Flint water crisis through a restorative justice lens by engaging the following questions: "Who was harmed in the Flint water crisis?" "What was the harm, or what harm was caused?" Patterson and Gray push further by asking *how* the harm was caused and *why*. And, finally, the classroom community generates ideas about what can be done to repair the harm and whether it is possible to seek justice to address the wrongdoing. In Gray's classroom, her students are positioned as "Scholars--Scientists--Warriors" which speaks to the work of TJTE in science education: who gets counted as a scientist, and how do race and ethnicity factor into which students are pursuing STEM (science, technology, engineering, and mathematics) coursework?[17]

There are also opportunities to address historical harm inflicted on communities of color in the name of science. Questions we ask science teachers to consider include the following:

- Who is science for and why?
- What is the role of "citizen science" in the classroom?[18]
- How can literature be used in the teaching of science?
- How can science address historical harms to communities of color in ethical ways?

Ultimately, TJTE science education scholars are asked "How can your class become part of a long arc of justice?" with the acknowledgment that this will be a "slow but urgent process."[19]

English Language Arts

When I introduced restorative English education in secondary schools, I presented *The Autobiography of Malcolm X* as a text that has transformed people's lives by showing the trajectories of Malcolm Little, Detroit Red, Malcolm X, and El-Hajj Malik El-Shabazz.[20] For many students, it was the first time they had seen glimpses of their past, present, and future selves on a printed page; they had never read a text that described anyone from what they perceived to be their own community. While the range of literature offered in some schools has expanded, there is a dearth of children's and young adult literature that features people of color as protagonists.[21] Why does this matter? Father and son children's literature and young adult literature authors Walter Dean Myers and Christopher Myers have discussed the effect of not having access to characters that reflect one's lived experiences in books. Walter Dean Myers recounted a rude awakening of sorts when he realized "something was missing" in the literature used in his school: "As I discovered who I was, a black teenager in a white-dominated world, I saw these characters, these lives, were not mine. I did not want to become the 'black' representative or some shining example of diversity. What I wanted, needed really, was to become an integral and valued part of the mosaic I saw around me."[22]

Digital tools create opportunities for students to find writing communities they may or may not find in classrooms or schools, allowing young learners to develop literate identities that are sustainable. Ebony Elizabeth Thomas and Amy Stornaiuolo have examined how young people engage in "textual justice" by "restorying" dominant narratives and inserting the faces, voices, and ideas that represent them.[23] In TJTE, we ask:

- Who gets to be a reader/writer/thinker/speaker in the English language arts classroom?
- How are you handling the single, monolithic stories of privileged groups and creating space for the complex lives and lived experiences of the students in your classroom?
- Who do we need to hear from? What voices/stories/perspectives are missing in our curriculum?

Literacy scholarship has been at the forefront of challenging the binaries of whose literacy matters, who gets counted as both literate and literary in education research.[24] I have found throughout my work that historical research, and ethnohistory in particular, is much needed to determine the "unexpected sources" in Indigenous, Black, Latinx, and multiply-minoritized communities.[25] TJTE scholars are concerned with not merely what it means to teach in the age of mass or hyper-incarceration but also "what it means to learn" in this time.[26]

Social Studies/History/Ethnic Studies

As with teachers of English language arts, social studies educators must resist monolithic stories that become "cultural logos" for students and their families. Efforts to establish ethnic studies programs across the country are a prime example of TJTE. Rather than asking why ethnic studies are appropriate or important, we begin with why there has been such backlash against ethnic studies. Arizona House Bill 2281 made it illegal to teach Mexican American studies in any public school in the state, but this move only galvanized a movement.[27] In addition to providing opportunities for youth to self-define and self-determine, ethnic studies provide students and educators with tools to identify race and racism and challenge institutional racism while actively resisting being silent and silenced. Ethnic studies initiatives have yielded compelling materials, such as a reader focused on California in *Our Stories in Our Voices*, that offer analyses on topics as diverse as the Vietnam War, Filipino identities, race and real estate, labor, and multiracial identities.[28]

As with literacy education, emerging technologies are being used with increasing effectiveness to challenge dominant narratives and fill in the holes of social studies and history curricula. Using a photovoice participatory methodology, Cati V. de los Rios engaged in a ten-month ethnographic study with Chicanx youth of Mexican descent. Participants created photovoice compositions about their experiences with ethnic studies curricula. Photovoice, in the context of this work, is the use of photography to document in agentive ways.[29] Another example of a TJTE in social studies/history in action is the work of classroom teacher Damany Fisher, whose "Race and Real Estate" curriculum examines why and how neighborhoods develop differently.[30] Fisher invites student to not only consider historical origins of neighborhoods but also engage in problem solving using documentary source records that reveal race restrictive covenants. Fisher also invites student to examine materials produced by the National Association of Real Estate Brokers. For a culminating project, students produce maps that historicize the development (or underdevelopment) of neighborhoods in their cities.

While these are examples of pedagogical stances at work in restorative justice work with children and youth both in school and in out-of-school contexts, much of this work is unfolding. Some questions for students and teachers across disciplines to consider include:

- Why ethnic studies? Why now?
- How can social studies/history create a participatory culture in classroom and school communities?
- What is the role of social studies/history classrooms in cultivating purpose and belonging for all students?
- This work cannot fall on the shoulders of social studies/history teachers. All teachers are responsible for engaging history. In order for restorative justice to be "embodied" in a classroom, as opposed to "thrown in," historicizing work must be done across disciplines.[31]

WHY "JUSTICE" IS A CRUCIAL COMPONENT OF TRANSFORMATIVE JUSTICE TEACHER EDUCATION

I was guilty of omitting the concept of "justice" from earlier iterations of this work. As a language and literacy scholar, I initially thought about the intersections of restorative justice and education solely though the lenses of literacy and English education. In 2013 I published a conceptual essay, "Toward a Restorative English Education," in which I defined restorative English education as "a pedagogy of possibilities" seeking to "resist zero-tolerance policies that sort, label, and eventually isolate particular youth."[32] I called on English, literacy, and writing educators, as well as teacher educators, to use their curricular powers and the mediating tools of poetry, prose, plays, memoirs, dialogue, and others to cultivate community and transform learners by building empathy and ensuring that diverse images and experiences in the curriculum resonate with students in personal ways. I rushed to provide tools and attempted to map how classroom teachers could borrow the compelling peacemaking and peacekeeping circle processes and conferences practiced by First Nations people in Canada; Maori communities in New Zealand; and Indigenous communities throughout the United States, such as the Ottawa, Chippewa, and Navaho, as well as similar processes embedded in African-centered practices.[33] In my haste to provide educators and teacher educators with a framework and list of things to do, I left "justice" behind.

As recently as 2016, I argued for restorative teacher education, for teacher education programs and preservice teachers to grapple with what it means to teach in the age of mass incarceration and the criminalization of Black, Latinx, Indigenous, differently abled, Muslim, LGBTQIQ, immigrant, and "undocumented" children, and their families. This reality has worsened and been exacerbated by increasingly public anti-Black/Brown sentiments and actions since the 2016 United States presidential election. As I continued to think about this work and how I could become a paradigm shift communicator, as charged by my mentor, sujatha baliga, I came to believe that omitting the concept of justice changed the meaning and purpose of this work. I recall a conversation with restorative justice practitioner Millie Burns, back when I first started questioning the use of "restorative practices" in education:

MAISHA: When we lose "justice," I wonder if we lose the historical context of why we need this work in the first place.

MILLIE: As I listen to you, I feel conflicted. When we first started this work in the seventies, we used the word "justice." We could also talk about race more in the sixties and seventies than you can today. However, when the teachers hear the words "restorative justice," they feel limited by what they can do, because there is not always a clear "victim" or clear "offender." (April 7, 2015)

Though Millie's statement has remained with me, for many years I could not reconcile my desire to pay fidelity to restorative justice and my desire to give the teachers I trained and worked with something they could do right away. I see now that Millie was right. Many teachers express feeling locked into the notion of justice. An RJ practitioner in the San Francisco Bay Area told me that teachers she works with in schools believe the "justice" in "restorative justice" unfairly took something from students who were excelling academically and socially and gave it to students who were exhibiting antisocial behaviors. There are often calls to stop talking about racism—one of the barriers to true justice for all—and start doing something about racism. However, many of us do not have the tools or the critical vocabularies (see chapter 2) to even discuss racism, privilege, and implicit bias, so it is difficult to imagine a critical dialogue around justice.[34] Restorative justice circle processes give us an opportunity and an intergenerational way to learn together to talk about race, to develop these critical vocabularies and sociocritical literacies, and to begin the practice of valuing and using restorative justice discourses.

EPILOGUE

I have been thinking a lot about trees. Yes, trees. Trying to take a break from this work, I decided to read *The Hidden Life of Trees: What They Feel, How They Communicate.*[1] I followed Peter Wohlleben, forester turned environmentalist, into the Eifel Mountains in Germany, where he manages beech and oak trees, and I suddenly returned to the work of restorative justice. Acknowledging the limitations of his early career as a forester concerned with trees' "suitability for the lumber mill and their market value," Wohlleben began to focus on how trees experience the world: "When you know that trees experience pain and have memories and that tree parents live together with their children, then you can no longer just chop them down and disrupt their lives with large machines."[2]

Wohlleben's paradigm shifted from thinking about the value of a tree for the sake of consumption to recognizing that trees relate to and support one another—much like the shift educators must make in schools that need to be restored (or, in most cases, transformed) into learning communities where all students and educators can thrive. Wohlleben began to ask why trees were such social beings after he learned about their interdependence and how root systems keep them connected. His conclusion was that trees are social creations for the same reasons humans tend to seek community: "There are advantages to working together. A tree is not a forest. On its own a tree cannot establish a consistent local climate . . . To get to this point, the community must remain intact no matter what. If every tree were looking out only for itself, then quite a few of them would never reach old age . . . Every tree, therefore, is valuable to the community and worth keeping around for as long as possible."[3]

I want to hold on to Wohlleben's statement that a tree is not a forest. In this book I reference the work of Fania Davis, former civil rights trial lawyer and cofounder and co-executive director of Restorative Justice for Oakland Youth. Davis has a similar way of describing the work of restorative justice: she positions everyone as part of an interconnected web; if any part of the web becomes damaged, we need to figure out how to repair it. Davis called for a truth and reconciliation process in the United States as an ethical response to violence against Black and Brown people after eighteen-year-old Michael Brown was murdered by police officers in the streets of Ferguson, Missouri, a tragedy that was followed by the murders of more innocent young men and women of color.[4] Dr. Martin Luther King Jr.'s well-known teachings from his "Letter from Birmingham Jail" caution and remind us all that "a threat to justice anywhere is a threat to justice everywhere. We are caught in an inescapable network of mutuality tied in a single garment of destiny. Whatever affects one directly affects all indirectly."[5] When we fail to address the harms and needs impacting our children and youth and refuse to assign responsibility for these obligations, we fail to prepare an entire generation to practice empathy, build healthy relationships amid and across difference, and, in too many cases, affirm the rights of anyone deemed "other."

As I competed this manuscript, a story was unfolding. A boy in Farmington Public Schools in Michigan chose not to stand during the Pledge of Allegiance—an intentional practice that both he and his father had enacted throughout the boy's years of schooling. While the facts of this story were being debated in the press, the boy's teacher was accused of "snatching" him out of his chair and subsequently placed on administrative leave. His father, a social worker in a nearby school district, noted that when he dropped his son off "into the hands of East Middle School," he expected "nurturing hands" and an environment where his son would feel "safe."[6] When the *Detroit Free Press* requested an interview, he further asserted, "How many kids would be such critical thinkers and leaders to be able to walk to their own beat and blaze their own path? He didn't follow anybody."[7] I, of course, thought about Kennedy High School and how educators encourage the student body to exercise thoughtful choice, even when the tinny loudspeaker tells them "We live in a nation of freedom."

If we engage in processes that allow us to listen to one another—really listen to one another, learn from one another, and elevate our awareness of context in our rich and textured lives—we begin the process and the practice of restoring justice. We owe this, at least, to our children.

NOTES

INTRODUCTION

1. Amy Davidson Sorkin, "What Niya Kenny Saw," *New Yorker*, October 30, 2015, https://www.newyorker.com/news/amy-davidson/what-niya-kenny-saw.
2. WIS Staff, "FBI to Lead Investigation of Violent Incident at Spring Valley High School," November 19, 2015, http://www.wistv.com/story/30353999/fbi-to-lead-investigation-of-violent-incident-at-spring-valley-high-school.
3. Sorkin, "What Niya Kenny Saw."
4. South Carolina Code of Laws Unannotated, Title 16: Crimes and Offenses, Chapter 17, Article 7, Section16-17-420, South Carolina Legislature, https://www.scstatehouse.gov/code/t16c017.php. The American Civil Liberties Union filed a complaint in 2016, *Kenny v. Wilson*, to challenge the "Disturbing Schools" statute, arguing that it "violates fundamental concepts of fairness and the most basic tenets of due process"; see https://www.aclu.org/legal-document/kenny-v-wilson-complaint.
5. See AB 420 Pupil discipline: suspensions and expulsions: willful defiance, California Legislative Information, https://leginfo.legislature.ca.gov/faces/billNavClient.xhtml?bill_id=201320140AB420.
6. All student and teacher names in this book are pseudonyms.
7. Kay Pranis, "The Restorative Impulse," *Tikkun* (Winter 2012): 33–34.
8. Marcus Hung, "Talking Circles Promote Equitable Discourse," *Mathematics Teacher* 109, no. 4 (2015): 256–60.
9. Ibid., 258.

10. Elizabeth Green, "Why Do Americans Stink at Math?" *New York Times*, July 23, 2014.
11. Mathematics professor and researcher Erika D. Bullock discusses the Spring Valley High incident in her work on math equity, arguing that teachers across disciplines—especially mathematics—must consider the role of harsh discipline policies and access to higher-level mathematics for students of color.
12. For three days, small groups of no more than twenty personnel participate in RJ circle facilitation training, responding to questions such as "When you were a kid, what did you want to be when you grew up?" and "Who was your favorite person at your school and why?" Eventually the questions guide participants to reflect on themselves as students by asking "Who were you at your best as a student?" "Who were you at your worst as a student?" "How are you like your/the students?" and "How are you different?" In the third segment, personnel respond to statements such as "Describe a time when race mattered to you" and "Describe a time when someone described you or someone you cared about in terms that were negative or demeaning."
13. Howard Zehr, *The Little Book of Restorative Justice* (Intercourse, PA: Goodbooks, 2002), 68.
14. Ta-Nehisi Coates, "Letter to My Son," *Atlantic* (July 4, 2015); adapted from Coates, *Between the World and Me* (New York: Spiegel & Grau, 2015).
15. Garrett Duncan, "Urban Pedagogies and the Celling of Adolescents of Color," *Social Justice*, 27, no. 3 (2000): 29–42.
16. Marc Lamont Hill, *Nobody: Casualties of America's War on the Vulnerable, from Ferguson to Flint and Beyond* (New York: Atria Publishing Group, 2016).
17. Pranis, "Restorative Impulse," 34.
18. See "Civil Rights Data Collection: Data Snapshot (School Discipline)," US Department of Education Office for Civil Rights, March 21, 2014, https://www2.ed.gov/about/offices/list/ocr/docs/crdc-discipline-snapshot.pdf.

19. Maisha T. Winn and Nadia Behizadeh, "The Right to Be Literate: Literacy, Education, and the School-to-Prison Pipeline," *Review of Research in Education* 35, no. 1 (2011): 147–73.
20. See Civil Rights Data Collection, "Restraint and Seclusion," 9.
21. William Haft, "More Than Zero: The Cost of Zero Tolerance and the Case for Restorative Justice in Schools," *Denver University Law Review* 77 (2000): 795.
22. Louis Mercer, "Detention of a Different Kind: Police, Chicago's Schools, and the Origins of the School-to-Prison Pipeline" (Spencer Dissertation Fellows presentation, Washington, DC, Fall 2016).
23. Howard Zehr, *Changing Lenses: Restorative Justice for Our Times*, 25th Anniversary Edition (Harrisonburg, VA: Herald Press, 2015).
24. Fania Davis, "This Country Needs a Truth and Reconciliation Process on Violence against African Americans—Right Now," *Yes! Magazine*, July 8, 2016, http://www.yesmagazine.org/peace-justice/this-country-needs-a-truth-and-reconciliation-process-on-violence-against-african-americans.

CHAPTER 1

1. These women choose a lowercase name format because, in the spirit of bell hooks, they wish to convey that the substance of their work is important, not their personal identities, and they feel that this more casual format better represents their personal approach to their work.
2. See Paul Tullis, "Can Forgiveness Play a Role in Criminal Justice?" *New York Times Magazine*, January 4, 2013.
3. Personal communication, March 5, 2015.
4. Maisha T. Winn, "We Are All Prisoners: Privileging Prison Voices in Black Print Culture," *Journal of African American History* 95, nos. 3–4 (2010): 392–416.
5. Howard Zehr, *The Little Book of Restorative Justice* (Intercourse, PA: Goodbooks, 2002), 22–24.
6. Damien Schnyder, "Enclosures Abound: Black Cultural Autonomy, Prison Regime, and Public Education," in *Education and*

Incarceration, ed. Erica R. Meiners and Maisha T. Winn (New York: Routledge, 2012), 77.

7. Ibid.
8. Fania Davis, "This Country Needs a Truth and Reconciliation Process on Violence against African Americans—Right Now," *Yes! Magazine,* July 8, 2016, http://www.yesmagazine.org/peace-justice/this-country-needs-a-truth-and-reconciliation-process-on-violence-against-african-americans.
9. Maisha T. Winn, "Transforming Justice. Transforming Teacher Education" (working paper, TeachingWorks, University of Michigan, Ann Arbor, 2016).
10. K. Wayne Yang, "Discipline or Punish? Some Suggestions for School Policy and Teacher Practices," *Language Arts* 87, no. 1 (2009): 51.
11. Zehr, *Little Book*, 24.
12. It is important to note that there are scholars in human rights education who assert that the field has values that are similar to those of restorative justice. See Maria Hantzopoulos, *Dignity in Public Schools: Human Rights Education in Action* (New York: Teacher College Press, 2016).
13. William Haft, "More Than Zero: The Cost of Zero Tolerance and the Case for Restorative Justice in Schools," *Denver University Law Review* 77 (2000): 795.
14. Ibid., 797.
15. Sonia Jain, Henrissa Bassey, Martha A. Brown, and Preety Kalra, *Restorative Justice in Oakland Schools: Implementation and Impacts* (Oakland, CA: Office for Civil Rights, US Department of Education, 2014), v.
16. During the 2015–2016 academic year, FUSD reported 73,460 students; of those students, 49,341 identified as "Hispanic/Latino."
17. Mackenzie Mays, "Restorative Justice? Teachers Say McLane High Classrooms Are Spiraling Out of Control," *Fresno Bee*, December 10, 2016.
18. Ibid.

19. Molly Beck, "Madison Teachers: New Discipline Policies Not Working," *Wisconsin State Journal*, October 28, 2014.
20. Susan Dominus, "An Effective but Exhausting Alternative to High-School Suspensions," *New York Times Magazine*, September 7, 2016, https://www.nytimes.com/2016/09/11/magazine/an-effective-ut-exhausting-alternative-to-high-school-suspensions.html.
21. Kennedy High School is a pseudonym.

CHAPTER 2

1. See Dana Ford, Greg Botelho, and Kevin Conlon, "Spring Valley High School Officer Suspended after Violent Classroom Arrest," CNN, http://www.cnn.com/2015/10/27/us/south-carolina-school-arrest-video/index.html.
2. Minnesota Public Radio News, "Why Don't We Talk about Young Black Females?," September 25, 2013, https://www.mprnews.org/story/2013/09/25/daily-circuit-black-female-youth.
3. An African American girl, Desre'e Watson, was handcuffed after having a tantrum in her kindergarten class in Avon Park, Florida in 2007. According to the chief of police, the six-year-old "became violent . . . she was yelling, screaming—just being uncontrollable. Defiant." Bob Herbert, "6-Year-Olds Under Arrest," *New York Times*, April 9, 2007, http://www.nytimes.com/2007/04/09/opinion/09herbert.html.
4. Maisha T. Winn, "'Betwixt and Between': Literacy, Liminality, and the 'Celling' of Black Girls," *Race, Ethnicity, and Education* 13, no. 4 (2010): 425–47; Maisha T. Winn, "'Our Side of the Story': Moving Incarcerated Youth Voices from Margin to Center," *Race, Ethnicity, and Education* 13, no. 3 (2010): 313–25; Maisha T. Winn and Nadia Behizadeh, "The Right to Be Literate: Literacy, Education, and the School-to-Prison Pipeline," *Review of Research in Education* 35, no. 1 (2011): 147–73; Maisha T. Winn, "The Politics of Desire and Possibility in Urban Playwriting: (Re)reading and (Re)writing the Script," *Pedagogies: An International Journal* 7, no. 4 (2012): 317–32.

5. John L. Jackson, *Thin Description: Ethnography and the African Hebrew Israelites of Jerusalem* (Cambridge, MA: Harvard University Press, 2013), 7.
6. Angela Y. Davis, *Freedom Is a Constant Struggle: Ferguson, Palestine, and the Foundations of a Movement* (Chicago: Haymarket Books, 2016).
7. Mariana Souto-Manning, "Critical Narrative Analysis: The Interplay of Critical Discourse and Narrative Analysis," *International Journal of Qualitative Studies in Education* 27, no. 2 (2014): 159–80.
8. Richard Fausset, Richard Pérez-Peña, and Alan Blinder, "Race and Discipline in Spotlight after South Carolina Officer Drags Student," *New York Times*, October 27, 2015, https://www.nytimes.com/2015/10/28/us/spring-valley-high-school-sc-officer-arrest.html.
9. Bryan Stevenson, *Just Mercy* (New York: Spiegel & Grau, 2014).
10. May Wong, "Bryan Stevenson Highlights Racism, Inequity in Criminal Justice System in Stanford Talk," Stanford University News, January 15, 2016, https://news.stanford.edu/2016/01/15/openxchange-stevenson-panel-011516.
11. Angela Y. Davis, *The Meaning of Freedom and Other Difficult Dialogues* (San Francisco: City Lights, 2012), 185.
12. The Equal Justice Initiative, a nonprofit organization that assists in helping wrongfully convicted prisoners achieve justice, is constructing a racial justice museum in Montgomery, Alabama, and launched an exhibit titled "The Legacy of Lynching" at the Brooklyn Museum in the summer of 2017.
13. Ibram X. Kendi, *Stamped from the Beginning: The Definitive History of Racist Ideas in America* (New York: Nation Books, 2016), 11.
14. Vanessa Siddle Walker, *Their Highest Potential: An African American School Community in the Segregated South* (Chapel Hill: University of North Carolina Press, 1996); Vanessa Siddle Walker and Renarta H. Tompkins, "Caring in the Past: The Case of a Southern Segregated African American School," in *Race-ing Moral Formation: African American Perspectives on Care*, ed. Vanessa Siddle Walker and John R. Snarey (New York: Teachers College Press, 2004), 77–92.

15. Vanessa Siddle Walker, "Second-Class Integration: A Historical Perspective for a Contemporary Agenda," *Harvard Educational Review* 79, no. 2 (2009): 269–84.
16. Garrett Duncan, "Urban Pedagogies and the Celling of Adolescents of Color," *Social Justice*, 27, no. 3 (2000): 29–42; P. D. Quijada Cerecer, "The Policing/Ruling of Native Bodies and Minds: Perspective Schooling from American Indian Youth," *American Journal of Education* 119, no. 4 (2013): 591–616; Monique Morris, *Pushout: The Criminalization of Black Girls in Schools* (New York: New Press, 2016).
17. Gloria Ladson-Billings, "Justice . . . Just Justice!," Social Justice in Education Lecture, American Educational Research Association Annual Meeting, Chicago, Illinois, April 16, 2015.
18. Davis, *Freedom Is a Constant Struggle*, 89.
19. Robin D. G. Kelley, foreword to *The Meaning of Freedom* (San Francisco: City Lights, 2012), 7.
20. Maisha T. Fisher, *Writing in Rhythm: Spoken Word Poetry in Urban Classrooms*, Language and Literacy Series (New York: Teachers College Press, 2007); Maisha T. Fisher, "Literocracy: Liberating Language and Creating Possibilities," *English Education* 37, no. 2 (2005): 92–95; Maisha T. Fisher, "From the Coffee House to the School House: The Promise and Potential of Spoken Word Poetry in School Contexts," *English Education* 37, no. 2 (2005): 115–31. The Power Writers class is a collective of youth poets and writers that was initially started by Joseph Ubiles at University Heights High School in the Bronx before becoming a nonprofit organization.
21. Winn, "Betwixt and Between"; Winn, "Our Side of the Story"; Winn and Behizadeh, "Right to Be Literate"; Winn, "Politics of Desire." Girl Time, founded by a woman-focused theater company, provided playwriting and acting workshops to incarcerated and formerly incarcerated girls.
22. Maisha T. Fisher, *Black Literate Lives: Historical and Contemporary Perspectives*, Critical Social Thought Series (New York: Routledge, 2009).

23. Carla Shalaby, *Troublemakers: Lessons in Freedom from Young Children at School* (New York: New Press, 2017), xvii; Mica Pollock, *Schooltalk: Rethinking What We Say About—and to—Students Every Day* (New York: New Press, 2017).
24. Howard Zehr, *Changing Lenses: Restorative Justice for Our Times*, 25th Anniversary Edition (Harrisonburg, VA: Herald Press, 2015), 241.
25. Gloria Ladson-Billings, "Reading, Writing, and Race: Literacy Practices of Teachers in Diverse Classrooms," in *Language, Literacy, and Power in Schooling*, ed. T. L. McCarty (Mahwah, NJ: Lawrence Erlbaum, 2005), 133–50.
26. Davis, *Meaning of Freedom*, 181–82.
27. Howard Zehr, *The Little Book of Restorative Justice* (Intercourse, PA: Goodbooks, 2002), 22–24.
28. Shawn Ginwright, "The Beautiful Struggle" (keynote address at the UC Davis Equity Summit, University of California, Davis, March 21, 2017).
29. Maisha T. Winn, "Toward a Restorative English Education," *Research in the Teaching of English* 48, no. 1 (2013): 126–35.
30. Zehr, *Changing Lenses*, 240.
31. Kris Gutiérrez, "Language and Literacies as Civil Rights," in *Literacy as a Civil Right: Reclaiming Social Justice in Literacy Research*, ed. Stuart Greene (New York: Peter Lang, 2008), 169.
32. The talking piece gets passed to everyone and people always reserve the right to pass. Depending on who trains the facilitator, the talking piece is passed either clockwise or counter-clockwise.
33. Michael White, *Maps of Narrative Practice* (New York: W. W. Norton, 2007); Michael White and David Epston, *Narrative Means to Therapeutic Ends* (New York: W. W. Norton, 1990).
34. Emily Watt, "A History of Youth Justice in New Zealand" (research paper, New Zealand, Department for Courts, 2003).
35. Specifically, Bazemore and Schiff assert that the United Nations' *Declaration on the Rights of Indigenous Peoples* provides important principles such as "self-determination" that are central to restorative justice work. Gordon Bazemore and Mara Schiff, "Understanding

Restorative Community Justice: What and Why Now?," in *Restorative Community Justice: Repairing Harm and Transforming Communities*, ed. Gordon Bazemore and Mara Schiff (Cincinnati, OH: Anderson Publishing, 2001), 21–46. For other examples of circle work across communities, see Melanie Spiteri, "Sentencing Circles for Aboriginal Offenders in Canada: Furthering the Idea of Aboriginal Justice within a Western Justice Framework" (master's thesis, University of Windsor, 2002).

36. Kay Pranis, *The Little Book of Circle Processes: A New/Old Approach to Peacemaking* (Intercourse PA: Good Books, 2005), 24.
37. US Committee on the Judiciary, *Ending the School-to-Prison Pipeline*, Hearing before the Committee on the Judiciary, United States Senate, One Hundred Twelfth Congress, Second Session, December 12, 2012, Serial No. J-112-95, https://www.gpo.gov/fdsys/pkg/CHRG-112shrg86166/pdf/CHRG-112shrg86166.pdf.
38. Gloria Ladson-Billings, "From the Achievement Gap to Educational Debt: Understanding Achievement in U.S. Schools, *Educational Researcher* 35, no. 7 (2006): 3–12; Maisha T. Winn, "Transforming Justice. Transforming Teacher Education" (working paper, TeachingWorks, University of Michigan, Ann Arbor, 2016).
39. Adam Gamoran, "Inequality Is the Problem—What's Our Response?," William T. Grant Foundation, July 1, 2014, http://wtgrantfoundation.org/inequality-is-the-problem-whats-our-response.
40. Ibid., 10.
41. Kelley, foreword to *The Meaning of Freedom*.
42. This section appears in my Spencer Invited Essay for the Lyle Spencer Grant.
43. Anna Stetsenko, "From Participation to Transformation: Implications of a Transformative Activist Stance for Human Development" (paper presented at the 4th Congress of the International Society for Cultural and Activity Research [ISCAR], Sydney, Australia, 2014).
44. Nai'lah Suad Nasir and Victoria M. Hand, "Exploring Sociocultural Perspectives on Race, Culture, and Learning," *Review of Research in Education* 76, no. 4 (2006): 465–75.

45. Stetsenko, "From Participation to Transformation."
46. Kay Pranis, "The Restorative Impulse," *Tikkun* (Winter 2012): 34.

CHAPTER 3

1. On the Southeast, see Maisha T. Winn, "'Betwixt and Between': Literacy, Liminality, and the 'Celling' of Black Girls," *Race, Ethnicity, and Education* 13, no. 4 (2010): 425–47; Maisha T. Winn, "'Our Side of the Story': Moving Incarcerated Youth Voices from Margin to Center," *Race, Ethnicity, and Education* 13, no. 3 (2010): 313–25; and Maisha T. Winn and Nadia Behizadeh, "The Right to Be Literate: Literacy, Education, and the School-to-Prison Pipeline," *Review of Research in Education* 35, no. 1 (2011): 147–73. On the Northeast, see Maisha T. Fisher, *Writing in Rhythm: Spoken Word Poetry in Urban Classrooms*, Language and Literacy Series (New York: Teachers College Press, 2007), and Maisha T. Winn, "*Still* Writing in Rhythm: Youth Poets at Work," *Urban Education* (April 11, 2016).
2. Annie E. Casey Foundation rankings were compiled for 2014 based on an index that "compares how children are progressing on key milestones across racial and ethnic groups at the national and state levels." "Race for Results Index Values, by Race and Ethnicity," Kids Count Data Center, http://datacenter.kidscount.org/data/tables/8060-race-for-results-index-values-by-race-and-ethnicity?loc=1&loct=1#detailed/2/2-9,11-52/false/869/4215,3301,4216,4218,4217/15486.
3. In fall 2013, Race to Equity published a baseline report of racial disparities among Blacks and Whites in the areas of education, criminal justice, workforce, and health care in Dane County, Wisconsin. This report fueled discussions, debates, and a great deal of civic engagement and action throughout the county.
4. TRANSFORM is a pseudonym.
5. I was unable to interview two of the recommended thirteen SCKs due to scheduling conflicts. My institutional review board protocol stipulated that I would not disrupt academic time (i.e., classes, academic enrichment, etc.).

6. While I am aware of the differences between "equality" (the state of being equal) and "equity" (what is "right" and "fair"), SCKs only used the word "equality" when discussing RJ circle processes.
7. Fisher, *Writing in Rhythm.*
8. Winn, "*Still* Writing in Rhythm."
9. Zeus Leonardo and Ronald K. Porter, "Toward a Fanonian Theory of 'Safety' in Race Dialogue," *Race, Ethnicity & Education* 13, no. 2 (2010): 139–57.
10. James Forman Jr., "Racial Critiques of Mass Incarceration: Beyond the New Jim Crow," *NYU Law Review* 87, no. 1 (2012): 101–146.
11. Maisha T. Winn, "We Are All Prisoners: Privileging Prison Voices in Black Print Culture," *Journal of African American History* 95, nos. 3–4 (2010): 392–416.
12. Erica Meiners, *Right to Be Hostile: Schools, Prisons, and the Making of Public Enemies* (Abingdon, UK: Taylor & Francis, 2007).
13. Fania Davis, "This Country Needs a Truth and Reconciliation Process on Violence against African Americans—Right Now," *Yes! Magazine,* July 8, 2016, http://www.yesmagazine.org/peace-justice/this-country-needs-a-truth-and-reconciliation-process-on-violence-against-african-americans.
14. Meiners, *Right to Be Hostile.*
15. Elise Jensen, *School-Based Youth Courts: Student Perceptions of School Climate, Safety, and Disciplinary Measures* (New York: Center for Court Innovation, 2015), 1.
16. Winn and Behizadeh, "Right to Be Literate."
17. Fisher, *Writing in Rhythm.*

CHAPTER 4

1. For more on pedagogical portraits, see Maisha T. Winn and Nadia Behizadeh, "The Right to Be Literate: Literacy, Education, and the School-to-Prison Pipeline," *Review of Research in Education* 35, no. 1 (2011): 147–73.
2. I spoke with Officer Gold several times, but because we were unable to get clearance, he could not grant me an official interview.

3. Maisha T. Winn and Joseph Ubiles, "Worthy Witnessing: Collaborative Research in Urban Classrooms, " in *Studying Diversity in Teacher Education*, ed. Arnetha Ball and Cynthia Tyson (New York: Routledge, 2011), 295–308.
4. "Greeting Gateway" is a pseudonym.
5. I first learned about the usefulness of these questions from RJ practitioner Ananda Mirilli.
6. See Maisha T. Winn, "Transforming Justice. Transforming Teacher Education" (working paper, TeachingWorks, University of Michigan, Ann Arbor, 2016).
7. Minnesota is considered an early adopter of RJ paradigms in their criminal justice system and, more recently, in schools. See the work of Kay Pranis with the Minnesota Department of Corrections and Nancy Riestenberg with the Minnesota Department of Education.
8. This definition of a circle comes from Ted Wachtel, "Defining Restorative" (paper presented at Building a Worldwide Restorative Practices Learning Network, the 15th IIRP World Conference, Bethlehem, Pennsylvania, International Institute for Restorative Practices, 2013), 7; my italics. Several Kennedy staff members completed RJ training with the International Institute for Restorative Practices before and during my study.
9. Winn and Ubiles, "Worthy Witnessing."
10. Winn and Behizadeh, "Right to Be Literate"; Maisha T. Winn, "'Betwixt and Between': Literacy, Liminality, and the 'Celling' of Black Girls," *Race, Ethnicity, and Education* 13, no. 4 (2010): 425–47; Maisha T. Winn, "'Our Side of the Story': Moving Incarcerated Youth Voices from Margin to Center," *Race, Ethnicity, and Education* 13, no. 3 (2010): 313–25.

CHAPTER 5

1. Gloria T. Hull, Patricia Bell-Scott, and Barbara Smith, eds., *But Some of Us Are Brave: All the Women Are White, All the Blacks Are Men*, Black Women's Studies (New York: Feminist Press at the City University of New York, 1982), xviii.

2. Ibid., xxi.
3. Edward W. Morris, "'Ladies' or 'Loudies'? Perceptions and Experiences of Black Girls in Classrooms," *Youth & Society* 38, no. 4 (2007): 490–515; Maisha T. Winn, *Girl Time: Literacy, Justice, and the School-to-Prison Pipeline* (New York: Teachers College Press, 2011); Maisha T. Winn, "'Our Side of the Story': Moving Incarcerated Youth Voices from Margin to Center," *Race, Ethnicity, and Education* 13, no. 3 (2010): 313–25; Monique Morris, *Pushout*; Maisha T. Winn, "'Betwixt and Between': Literacy, Liminality, and the 'Celling' of Black Girls," *Race, Ethnicity, and Education* 13, no. 4 (2010): 425–47.
4. Jacqueline Jones, *Labor of Love, Labor of Sorrow: Black Women, Work, and the Family, from Slavery to Present* (Philadelphia: Basic Books, 2010), 5.
5. *Kenny v. Wilson* 2:16-cv-12794-CWH, South Carolina, was dismissed by a federal judge in 2017.
6. Rebecca Epstein, Jamila J. Blake, and Thalia González, "Girlhood Interrupted: The Erasure of Black Girls' Childhood" (report published by Georgetown Law Center on Poverty and Inequality, 2017), http://www.law.georgetown.edu/academics/centers-institutes/poverty-inequality/upload/girlhood-interrupted.pdf.
7. Erica Meiners, *For the Children? Protecting Innocence in a Carceral State* (Minneapolis: University of Minnesota Press, 2016).
8. Adam Gamoran, "Inequality Is the Problem: Prioritizing Research on Reducing Inequality" (annual report, William T. Grant Foundation, 2013), 10.
9. I do not wish to diminish vodou here. Part of my work as an ethnographer is to keep the language and naming practices of a community intact so I am quoting the teacher.

CHAPTER 6

1. Mary Rose O'Reilley, *The Peaceable Classroom* (Portsmouth, NH: Boynton/Cook Publishers, 1993).
2. Ibid., 9.

3. Shawn Ginwright, *Hope and Healing in Urban Education: How Urban Activists and Teachers Are Reclaiming Matters of the Heart* (New York: Routledge, 2016); Prudence L. Carter and Sean F. Reardon, "Inequality Matters" (William T. Grant Foundation Inequality Paper, 2014).
4. Michael J. Dumas, "'Losing an Arm': Schooling as a Site of Black Suffering," *Race, Ethnicity, and Education* 17, no. 1 (2014): 1–29.
5. Howard Zehr, *The Little Book of Restorative Justice* (Intercourse, PA: Goodbooks, 2002), 10.
6. Maisha T. Fisher, *Black Literate Lives: Historical and Contemporary Perspectives*, Critical Social Thought Series (New York: Routledge, 2009).
7. Oakland Unified School District News, "Restorative Welcome and Reentry Circle," April 26, 2013, https://www.youtube.com/watch?v=HiLtFVHR8Q0.
8. Erika C. Bullock, "Tracing Equity in Mathematics Education: (Re) imagining the Sociopolitical Turn" (lecture presented at the University of Wisconsin–Madison, May 2016).
9. Kobi Yamada, *What Do You Do with a Problem?* (Seattle, WA: Compendium Books, 2016).
10. Dawood Bey, *Class Pictures* (New York: Aperture Foundation, 2007).
11. H. Richard Milner IV, *Start Where You Are, but Don't Stay There: Understanding Diversity, Opportunity Gaps, and Teaching in Today's Classrooms* (Cambridge, MA: Harvard Education Press, 2015).
12. In October 2017 a community of practitioners and scholars from various schools, organizations, and universities throughout the United States participated in the "Toward a Transformative Justice Teacher Education" research convening hosted by the Transformative Justice in Education (TJE) Center in the School of Education at the University of California, Davis. The purpose of this convening, funded by the Spencer Foundation, was to launch what a TJTE looked like, felt like, and sounded like across disciplines. Participants included Subini Annamma, Kelly Jeanne Baker, Melissa Braaten, Bryan Brown, Erika Bullock, Patrick Camangian, Asha Canady, Roger Viet Chung, Damany Fisher, Sarah Warshauer Freedman, Rhoda Freelon,

Ashley George, Maisie Gholson, Salina Gray, Fahima Ife, Chelsea Jackson Roberts, Rita Kohli, Danny Martinez, Maxine McKinney de Royston, Erica R. Meiners, Elizabeth Montaño, Adam Musser, Alexis Patterson, Patricia Quijada, Cati de los Rios, Mariana Souto-Manning, Maya Sudarkalsa, Rayna Velasquez, Lawrence T. Winn, and Maisha T. Winn.

13. Danny B. Martin, Maisie Gholson, and Jacqueline Leonard, "Mathematics as Gatekeeper: Power and Privilege in the Production of Knowledge," *Journal of Urban Mathematics Education* 16 (December 2010): 16–17.
14. Myosha Macafee, "The Kinesiology of Race," *Harvard Educational Review* 84, no. 4 (2014): 468–91.
15. Erika C. Bullock, Maisie L. Gholson, Erica Meiners, Maxine McKinney de Royston, and Kellie Jeanne Baker, "Transformative Justice in Mathematics" (presented at the "Toward a Transformative Justice Teacher Education" research convening, Transformative Justice in Education (TJE) Center, University of California, Davis, October 2017).
16. Alexis Patterson and Salina Gray, "Chemistry Is Around Us: The Story of Flint" (teaching demonstration presented at the "Toward a Transformative Justice Teacher Education" research convening, Transformative Justice in Education Center, University of California, Davis, October 2017).
17. Bryan A. Brown, J. Bryan Henderson, Salina Gray, Brian Donovan, and Shayna Sullivan, "From Access to Success: Identity Contingencies and African-American Pathways to Science," *Higher Education Studies* 3, no. 1 (2013): 1–13.
18. The Center for Community and Citizen Science in the School of Education at the University of California, Davis, is taking on projects that demonstrate the impact of environmental science learning on conservation work. See Heidi Ballard, Collin G. H. Dixon, and Emily M. Harris, "Youth-Focused Citizen Science: Examining the Role of Environmental Science Learning and Agency for Conservation," *Biological Conservation* 208 (April 2017): 65–75.

19. Alexis Patterson, De Scipio, Melissa Braaten, Salina Gray, Rhoda Freelon, and Bryan Brown, "What Do We Think Teachers Need to Know/Do/Learn in Order to Teach Science in a Way That Stops Killing?" (presented at the "Toward a Transformative Justice Teacher Education" research convening, Transformative Justice in Education Center, University of California, Davis, October 2017).
20. Malcolm X, with Alex Haley, *The Autobiography of Malcolm X* (New York: Grove Press, 1965); Maisha T. Winn, "Toward a Restorative English Education," *Research in the Teaching of English* 48, no. 1 (2013): 126–35.
21. K. T. Horning, "I See White People," Cooperative Children's Book Center, CCBlogC, July 11, 2013; Cooperative Children's Book Center, "Publishing Statistics on Children's Books about People of Color and First/Native Nations and by People of Color and First/Native Nations Authors and Illustrators," Madison, Wisconsin, 2014, http://ccblogc.blogspot.com/2013/07/i-see-white-people.html; Walter Dean Myers, "Where Are the People of Color in Children's Books?" *New York Times*, March 15, 2014; Christopher Myers, "The Apartheid of Children's Literature," *New York Times*, March 15, 2014.
22. Myers, "Where Are the People of Color?"
23. Ebony Elizabeth Thomas and Amy Stornaiuolo, "Restorying the Self: Bending toward Textual Justice," *Harvard Educational Review* 86, no. 3 (2016): 313–36.
24. See Carol D. Lee, *Culture, Literacy, and Learning: Taking Bloom in the Midst of the Whirlwind* (New York: Teachers College Press, 2007); Carol D. Lee "Every goodbye ain't gone': Analyzing the Cultural Underpinnings of Classroom Talk," *International Journal of Qualitative Studies in Education* 19, no. 3 (2006): 305–327; Carol D. Lee, "A Culturally Based Cognitive Apprenticeship: Teaching African American High School Students Skills in Literary Interpretation," *Reading Research Quarterly* 30, no. 4 (1995): 608–629; Arnetha Ball, "Text Design Patterns in the Writing of Urban African American Students: Teaching to the Cultural Strengths of Students in Multicultural Settings," *Urban Education* 30, no. 3 (1995): 253–89; Kris D. Gutiérrez,

"Developing a Sociocritical Literacy in the Third Space," *Reading Research Quarterly* 43, no. 2 (2008): 148–64.

25. See Maisha T. Fisher, *Black Literate Lives: Historical and Contemporary Perspectives* (New York: Routledge, 2009). Here I extend Elizabeth McHenry's notion that the history of Black writers, readers, and speakers is still unfolding by examining the literate practices of poets and activists in the Black Power and Black Arts movements.
26. Patrick Camangian, Asha Canady, Cati de los Rios, Fahima Ife, Danny Martinez, Adam Musser, and Patricia Quijada Cerecer, "Toward Humanizing and Critical Translingual Approaches" (presented at the "Toward a Transformative Justice Teacher Education" research convening, Transformative Justice in Education Center, University of California, Davis, October 2017.
27. Cati V. de los Rios, "Picturing Ethnic Studies: Photovoice and Youth Literacies of Social Action," *Journal of Adult and Adolescent Literacy* 61, no. 1 (2017): 15–24.
28. Dale Allender and Gregory Y. Mark, eds. *Our Stories in Our Voices* (Dubuque, IA: Kendall Hunt Publishing, 2017).
29. Photovoice is a research methodology used in Participatory Action Research and Youth Participatory Research (as well as other community research approaches) where people can document their communities and raise issues with policy makers and local or national politicians.
30. Damany M. Fisher, "Race and Real Estate" (teaching demonstration presented at the "Toward a Transformative Justice Teacher Education" research convening, Transformative Justice in Education Center, University of California, Davis, October 2017).
31. Roger V. Chung, Damany M. Fisher, Sarah Warshauer Freedman, Rita Kohli, Elizabeth Montano and Maya Sudarkasa, "Transformative Justice Teacher Education in and Beyond Social Sciences" (presented at the "Toward a Transformative Justice Teacher Education" research convening, Transformative Justice in Education Center, University of California, Davis, October 2017).
32. Winn, "Toward a Restorative English Education."

33. Jessica Metoui, "Returning to the Circle: The Reemergence of Traditional Dispute Resolution in Native American Communities," no. 2 (2007), art. 6; Vera Nobles and Wade Nobles, "Serudja Ta: African-Centered Ideas about Humanness and Restoration: The Unfinished Revolution" (paper presented at the sixth National Association for Community Restorative Justice conference, Oakland, California, June 16, 2017).
34. Angela Y. Davis, *Freedom Is a Constant Struggle: Ferguson, Palestine, and the Foundations of a Movement* (Chicago: Haymarket Books, 2016), 89.

EPILOGUE

1. Peter Wohlleben, *The Hidden Life of Trees: What They Feel, How They Communicate* (Berkeley, CA: Greystone Books, 2015).
2. Ibid., xiv.
3. Ibid., 4.
4. Fania Davis, "This Country Needs a Truth and Reconciliation Process on Violence against African Americans—Right Now," *Yes! Magazine*, July 8, 2016, http://www.yesmagazine.org/peace-justice/this-country-needs-a-truth-and-reconciliation-process-on-violence-against-african-americans.
5. Martin Luther King Jr., "Letter from Birmingham Jail," published as "The Negro Is Your Brother," *Atlantic Monthly* 212, no. 2 (1963): 78–88.
6. Carla Herreira, "Teacher Accused of Assaulting Student for Sitting during Pledge of Allegiance," *Huffington Post*, September 16, 2017.
7. Lori Higgins, "Farmington Hills Teacher Accused of Assaulting Student Who Sat during the Pledge," *Detroit Free Press*, September 15, 2017.

ACKNOWLEDGMENTS

My deepest gratitude to the Hill Patwin and the River Patwin people of Yolo County, whose land I live, dream, and work on every day.

I am certain that I would never have understood the scope of restorative justice work without my dear friend, mentor, and colleague, sujatha baliga. sujatha's teachings have transformed my life, the way I engage, and the way I ask to be engaged. Once you commit to "making things right," there is no other way. sujatha's directive that I become a "paradigm shift communicator," a task I take quite seriously, became the impetus for this book. sujatha's team, nuri nusrat and Sia Henry, not only welcomed me but also challenged me, asked difficult questions, and held me accountable. I am grateful to this community of justice seekers and all the work they do for humanity.

Rita Alfred and Millie Burns were among my first teachers in restorative justice; their respective trainings, "Repairing Harm" and "Restorative Justice and Trauma-Informed Practices," gave me new lenses that I wish I'd had when I was an elementary and high school classroom teacher. The Transformative Justice in Education (TJE) Center in the School of Education at the University of California, Davis, which I co-direct with my husband, Torry Winn, has also been vital to this project. TJE provides an intellectual home, and our summer research team, including Maya Sudarkasa, Jeremy Prim, and Adam Musser, kept me motivated.

A writing retreat in New York City with my dear colleagues Dr. Shameka Powell and Dr. Mariana Souto-Manning was the turning point that ultimately brought this manuscript to completion. During this trip I was so grateful that my sister Dr. Aleesha Taylor asked about my work and put me in touch with her friend Tawnya Fay Switzer, who is now my friend too. Thank you both for your critical and specific feedback and, most of all, your support. Tawnya, I appreciated "geeking out" with you over word choice and the spot-on "working mommy chronicles" we exchanged.

Fahima Ife and Hannah Graham served as research assistants on my projects and embraced the Transformative Justice Teacher Education vision when they worked for me in the Secondary English Program at the University of Wisconsin–Madison. Dr. Ife and Mrs. Graham's work with preservice teachers is unprecedented, and their individual programs of research will undoubtedly make this work better.

Several colleagues have graciously hosted me at their institutions and given me opportunities to further develop the ideas in this book: Rich Milner and his colleagues at the Center for Urban Education at the University of Pittsburgh; Deborah Loewenberg Ball and her colleagues at TeachingWorks at the University of Michigan; Dale Allender and his colleagues at California State University, Sacramento; and Patrick Camangian and his colleagues with the People's Education Movement in the San Francisco Bay Area. I am also indebted to practitioners and scholars with whom I regularly exchange ideas: Dr. Michele Hamilton, Teacher Can, Señora Velasquez, Sarah Freedman (the advisor who keeps on giving!), Carol D. Lee, Kris D. Gutiérrez, Erica R. Meiners, Shaun Harper, Danny Martinez, Alexis Patterson, Patricia Quijada, and colleagues at the University of Wisconsin–Madison and at the University of California, Davis. This work would not have been possible without the support of the Spencer Foundation (New Civics Program) and the William T. Grant Foundation (Distinguished Fellows).

My family makes numerous sacrifices for me to engage in this work. My sons, Obasi and Zafir, were unbelievably flexible when I moved them across the country so that I could work with colleagues at the National Council on Crime and Delinquency and Impact Justice in Oakland, California, in 2015. This meant leaving behind some truly amazing caretakers and the teachers at Preschool of the Arts in order to transition into the unknown. Fortunately, a powerful team of early childhood educators at Step One Preschool (Teacher Aaron, Teacher Thèrése, and Teacher Tess) had Obasi's back, and Zafir was in excellent hands with Ms. Kriscia. I absolutely could not be a scholar without the support of such thoughtful and committed early childhood educators who see the full humanity of their students. I am also indebted to two amazing mommy friends, Susana Casher and Lisa Wong Jackson, who became lifelines during that time as our sons (six between us!) became dear friends, the "CashJackWinn Boys."

When I worked myself into a tizzy, my sister Aliya Johnson firmly convinced me to get myself to a doctor (she also had to pick me up and actually get me there!). My husband, Torry, believed in my work and did a lot of heavy lifting, traveling between Madison and Oakland weekly as he completed coursework for his doctoral program. He read drafts of these chapters late at night, early in the morning, and on weekends. Of course, I could blame him for any mistakes that might appear and he would happily assume responsibility—but any errors are truly my own.

In closing, I must acknowledge my mother, the late Cheryl Ann Fisher, a true justice seeker who attempted to put people in dialogue early and often in order to build community. Before I had the words "restorative justice," I saw her values at work and her insistence that rather than throwing people away, we achieve the greatest ends when we hold them closer than ever.

ABOUT THE AUTHOR

MAISHA T. WINN is the Chancellor's Leadership Professor in the School of Education at the University of California, Davis, where she also co-directs (with Torry Winn) the Transformative Justice in Education (TJE) Center. Winn's program of research examines the relationships between language, literacy, justice, and school policies. She began her career in education as an elementary school teacher and eventually a high school English teacher. In 2012 she received the American Educational Research Association Early Career Award and in 2016 was named an American Educational Research Association Fellow. As a 2014 William T. Grant Distinguished Fellow, Winn shadowed restorative justice attorneys and practitioners in the West and Midwest. She is the author of several books, including *Writing in Rhythm: Spoken Word Poetry in Urban Schools* (published under her maiden name, "Fisher"); *Black Literate Lives: Historical and Contemporary Perspectives* (published under "Fisher"); *Writing Instruction in the Culturally Relevant Classroom* (with Latrise P. Johnson); and *Girl Time: Literacy, Justice, and the School-to-Prison Pipeline*; and coeditor of *Humanizing Research: Decolonizing Qualitative Research* (with Django Paris). She is also the author of numerous articles in journals such as *Review of Research in Education*; *Anthropology and Education Quarterly*; *International Journal of Qualitative Studies in Education*; *Race, Ethnicity and Education*; *Research in the Teaching of English*; *Race and Social Problems*; and *Harvard Educational Review*.

INDEX